African Traditions: Preserving through Pickles and Fermentation

Andrew Darren Steele

Published by Steele Andrew Darren, 2024.

While every precaution has been taken in the preparation of this book, the publisher assumes no responsibility for errors or omissions, or for damages resulting from the use of the information contained herein.

AFRICAN TRADITIONS: PRESERVING THROUGH PICKLES AND FERMENTATION

First edition. March 28, 2024.

Copyright © 2024 Andrew Darren Steele.

ISBN: 979-8224098637

Written by Andrew Darren Steele.

Table of Contents

Introduction - The definition and classification of pickles and fermented foods in Africa

Pickles and fermented foods hold a significant place in African cuisine, adding flavor, texture, and nutritional value to various dishes. These foods undergo a process of preservation through fermentation, which not only enhances taste but also extends the shelf life of perishable ingredients.

Definition:

Pickles and fermented foods refer to a diverse array of food products in Africa, encompassing vegetables, fruits, grains, roots, and even dairy products that have been subjected to controlled microbial fermentation. This process converts the natural sugars into organic acids, often with the use of salt or a brine solution, creating a distinct taste and texture.

Types of Pickles and Fermented Foods:

1. Vegetable Pickles: In Africa, a wide range of vegetables are pickled, including cucumbers, green beans, carrots, onions, and various leafy greens like cabbage and kale. These vegetables are sometimes combined with spices, herbs, and chili peppers to achieve a unique flavor profile.

2. Fruity Chutneys: African chutneys are made by fermenting fruits like mangoes, guavas, and tomatoes. They are typically spicy and tangy, incorporating a mix of sweet and sour taste profiles. Chutneys are commonly consumed as condiments or accompaniments to main dishes.

3. Cereal-Based Fermented Foods: In many African countries, grains such as millet, sorghum, and maize are fermented to create staple foods. Examples include ogi or akamu, a fermented maize porridge; injera, a sourdough flatbread made from fermented teff flour; and burukutu, a traditional beer produced from fermented grains.

4. Dairy Fermentation: Several African cultures have a long history of fermenting dairy products such as milk, buttermilk, and yogurt. Traditional fermented dairy products include laban and kishk in North Africa, mahewu

in Southern Africa, and nunu in West Africa. These fermented dairy products offer unique tastes, textures, and beneficial microbial enzymes.

5. Fish and Meat Fermentation: Fermentation is also extensively used to preserve fish and meat in African cuisine. Examples include dried and salted fish, fermented fish paste (such as Nunu in Pedi culture), as well as processed and fermented meat products like biltong and droëwors in Southern Africa.

Classification:

When classifying pickles and fermented foods in Africa, several factors come into play:

1. Ingredients Used: They can be classified based on the primary ingredient: vegetables, fruits, cereals, dairy, fish, or meat.

2. Preparation Techniques: Different fermentation techniques are employed, such as spontaneous fermentation, back-slopping (using previously fermented ingredients), or the addition of starter cultures.

3. Regional Variations: African pickles and fermented foods can exhibit significant regional diversity due to variations in climate, local ingredients, and cultural traditions. Each region has unique flavors and methods of preparation.

4. Cultural Significance: Some recipes and techniques have cultural or religious significance. For example, Rwandan culture reveres traditional fermented beer, called urwagwa, used in rituals and festivities.

In conclusion, pickles and fermented foods form an integral part of African culinary traditions. With a multitude of types and methods of preparation, they provide a rich and diverse range of flavors, as well as preservation benefits that ensure food security. Exploring and embracing these foods allow for a deeper appreciation of the vast and vibrant African gastronomic heritage.

- The history and culture of pickles and fermented foods in Africa

The Rich History and Cultural Significance of Pickles and Fermented Foods in Africa

---

PICKLES AND FERMENTED foods have deep roots in African culinary history, representing a fascinating facet of the continent's diverse food culture. With a long-standing tradition that predates colonial influences, Africa's pickling and fermentation practices offer a unique insight into the continent's culinary heritage. In this article, we will delve into the history and cultural significance of pickles and fermented foods across Africa, highlighting their traditional methods, regional variations, and social importance.

1. Historical Origins:

The art of pickling and fermentation can be traced back to ancient times in Africa. Archaeological evidence suggests the use of fermented foods in Africa, with pottery jars containing remains of millet beer and fermented honey found in Sudan dating back thousands of years. These findings highlight the long-standing Ethiopian practices of fermenting grains and producing traditional alcoholic beverages like tej.

2. Traditional Fermented Foods:

A diverse range of fermented foods exists across the continent, reflecting the abundant regional biodiversity of Africa's crops. Specially prepared cassava, known as "fufu" or "gari," is a common staple in West and Central Africa, created by fermenting and processing the tubers. Similarly, different maize and sorghum porridges are fermented to create "ugali" or "pap," a popular dish in Eastern, Southern, and parts of West Africa.

Additionally, a variety of vegetables, ranging from cabbage, carrots, and chilies to cucumbers and Okra, are preserved using traditional pickling methods. These pickles often acquire unique flavors by incorporating local spices like ginger, coriander, or garlic.

3. Cultural Significance and Traditional Practices:

Pickling and fermentation traditionally play a crucial role in preserving surplus crops and extending their shelf life, enabling communities to maintain a steady food supply year-round. These methods have become an integral aspect of many African ethnic groups' culinary traditions, connecting people to their ancestral roots and strengthening community ties. Fermentation also contributes to the cultural fabric of various societies by becoming a source of exchange, gifts, or in celebration during social gatherings and festivals.

4. Regional Variations and Culinary Delights:

Different regions in Africa have unique methods of pickling and fermenting foods. For instance, in West Africa, "dawadawa" or "ogiri" is prepared from fermented locust beans, creating an umami-rich flavoring agent used in soups and stews. In Central Africa, "acheke" or "attieke" is a fermented cassava couscous enjoyed with various meat or vegetable dishes. Similarly, South Africa is renowned for pickled fish, commonly savored during the Easter season, while Ethiopia is famed for its fermented sourdough bread, injera, a staple in the country's cuisine.

5. Health Benefits and Science:

Beyond its cultural significance, fermented foods offer numerous health benefits. Lactic acid bacterial fermentation enhances digestibility, increases vitamin levels, and promotes the growth of beneficial bacterial strains in the intestinal microbiota. Additionally, pickled and fermented foods like kimchi and sauerkraut contribute to boosting the immune system due to their probiotic properties.

***

EXPLORING THE HISTORY and cultural significance of pickles and fermented foods in Africa reveals the depth of culinary heritage in the continent. From fermented porridges to pickled vegetables, these traditional preservation methods speak volumes about regional diversity, sustainable practices, and social bonding. Embracing these ancient techniques allows us to appreciate Africa's rich food culture and promotes the integration of healthy and probiotic foods in our daily lives.

- The main themes and objectives of the book

The main themes and objectives of the book represent the foundation upon which the entire narrative is constructed. They serve as guiding principles that shape the content and message of the story, and also provide readers with a deeper understanding of the author's intentions. By exploring these themes and objectives, readers can unravel the underlying meaning of the book and reflect upon its relevance to their own lives.

In some cases, the main themes of a book are evident from the very beginning and are seamlessly woven into the plot. For example, a novel may feature themes such as love, sacrifice, or redemption. These themes can be explored through the thoughts, actions, and relationships of the characters, offering readers various perspectives and insights. The author may also delve deeper into contemporary or timeless issues that affect society at large, such as discrimination, social inequality, or the destruction of the environment.

In contrast, the main objectives of a book may not be as explicitly apparent but still play a crucial role in its execution. These objectives often reflect the author's own motivations and aspirations for writing the book. One important objective could be to educate readers about a specific subject matter or historical event. Through thorough research and meticulous storytelling, an author can transmit valuable knowledge and inspire readers to delve deeper into the topic at hand. Another objective might be to convey moral lessons or provoke critical thinking, encouraging readers to reflect on their own values and beliefs.

Additionally, the book may strive to entertain and captivate its audience, employing elements of suspense, drama, or humor to create an engaging narrative. The author may aim to transport readers to new worlds, immersing them in richly descriptive settings and introducing them to memorable characters. By creating an emotional connection with readers and providing a powerful source of escapism, the book encourages an enjoyable and compelling reading experience.

Ultimately, the main themes and objectives of a book provide a framework that guides the author's creative decisions and serves to enrich the reader's understanding and appreciation of the story. They act as a backbone, offering both authors and readers a roadmap through the intricate layers of the narrative, while simultaneously creating a lasting impact on both the literary world and the readers' own lives.

Chapter 1: Pickled Fruits and Vegetables- The origin and distribution of pickled fruits and vegetables in Africa

Pickled fruits and vegetables are an essential part of African cuisine, adding unique flavors and enhancing the nutritional value of meals. In this chapter, we delve into the origin, historical significance, and distribution patterns of pickled fruits and vegetables in Africa.

Culinary Traditions:

Africa is a continent with a diverse range of culinary practices, each influenced by local ingredients, cultural traditions, and historical connections. The use of pickling techniques to preserve and enhance the flavor of fruits and vegetables has been an integral part of African cuisine for centuries.

Historical Significance:

Pickling has its roots in the ancient times, serving as a method to extend the shelf life of perishable produce. This preservation technique arose out of the necessity to store fruits and vegetables for times of scarcity, making it an integral part of African food culture.

Pickling has also played a crucial role in food security throughout history. In regions where access to fresh produce was limited, pickling fruits and vegetables provided a nutrient-rich alternative during seasons of scarcity. The practice allowed communities to sustain themselves with essential vitamins and minerals when fresh produce was not available.

Different Pickling Techniques:

Pickling methods in Africa vary by region, reflecting the abundance and diversity of local produce as well as cultural preferences. The traditional techniques can be broadly categorized into three categories: fermentation, vinegar-based, and salting.

In fermentation, fruits and vegetables are submerged in a brine solution containing salt and left to ferment over several days. This method not only preserves the produce but also introduces beneficial probiotics that boost gut health and contribute to the unique flavors of the pickles.

Vinegar-based pickles use acidic solutions to preserve the fruits and vegetables. The acidic nature of vinegar acts as a natural preservative, inhibiting the growth of microorganisms. The food items are soaked in vinegar, along with various spices and herbs, to infuse flavors and extend their shelf life.

Salting, another prevalent pickling technique, involves packing fruits and vegetables with salt or dry curing them to extract moisture. The dehydration process prevents spoilage and increases the longevity of the produce. Salt-preserved pickled fruits and vegetables are popular in coastal regions where salt harvesting is abundant.

Distribution Patterns:

The availability of pickled fruits and vegetables varies throughout Africa depending on regional preferences, climate, and indigenous plant species. Certain pickled fruits and vegetables are ubiquitous across the continent, while others have more limited distribution.

In North Africa, the traditional cuisine heavily relies on pickled olives, lemons, and cucumbers. Shatta, a spicy pepper paste, is also commonly consumed in this region as a side pickle and condiment.

In East Africa, pickled mangoes, chilies, and tamarind are prevalent. These flavorful pickles often accompany snacks and main dishes, adding a burst of tanginess.

Pickled okra, baobab fruits, and eggplants take center stage in the pickling traditions of West Africa. The mild tartness of pickled okra and the unique flavors of baobab fruits perfectly complement West African dishes.

The Southern region of Africa embraces pickles made from green or unripe fruits like tomatoes, pears, and plums. The inherent sourness of these fruits offers a refreshing and tangy twist to meals.

⸺⊙⸺

PICKLED FRUITS AND vegetables have a rich history and cultural significance in Africa. From their origin as a preservation technique to the diverse distribution patterns across the continent, pickles have become an essential component of African cuisine.

Understanding the origin and distribution of pickled fruits and vegetables in Africa allows us to appreciate the variations in flavors, techniques, and cultural significance attached to these culinary treasures. In the subsequent chapters, we will explore specific pickling recipes and their health benefits, enhancing our understanding and enjoyment of African cuisine.

- The ingredients and methods of making pickled fruits and vegetables in different ways

Pickling is a process of preserving fruits and vegetables by immersing them in a solution of vinegar, salt, and various spices. This age-old technique not only helps in extending the shelf life of these produce but also adds a tangy and flavorful twist to them. In this article, we will explore the ingredients and methods of making pickled fruits and vegetables in different ways, unveiling some unique and appetizing recipes.

1. Basic Ingredients:

The fundamental ingredients required for pickling are:

a) Fruits or Vegetables: While cucumbers are the most widely used for pickling, you can experiment with an array of other produce such as carrots, radishes, cauliflower, green beans, peppers, and even fruits like cherries and watermelon rinds.

b) Vinegar: Choose a vinegar with 5% acidity for safe and effective pickling. Commonly used types include white vinegar, apple cider vinegar, and rice vinegar (popular in Asian cuisine).

c) Salt: Use non-iodized salt, such as Kosher or sea salt, as iodized salt can affect the appearance and taste of the pickles.

d) Sweeteners (optional): Sugar or other sweeteners like honey, maple syrup, or even stevia can be added to balance out the tartness of vinegar.

e) Spices and Herbs: This is where you can get creative. Some popular choices include dill seed, mustard seed, garlic, peppercorns, bay leaves, cinnamon sticks, cloves, ginger, and red pepper flakes. Experiment with different combinations to achieve your desired flavor.

2. Traditional Pickling Method:

The traditional pickling method typically involves the following steps:

a) Brining: Prepare a brine solution by mixing 1 cup of vinegar, 1 cup of water, and 1 tablespoon of salt. Simmer this brine until the salt dissolves completely. Cool it before using.

b) Sterilization: Sterilize the jars and lids by washing them in hot, soapy water or by placing them in boiling water for a few minutes. This step ensures that harmful bacteria are eliminated.

c) Prepping the Produce: Wash and trim the fruits or vegetables, removing any blemishes. Cut them into the desired size and shape. For certain vegetables like cucumbers, a process called "curing" involving soaking them in an ice bath for a few hours is recommended to retain crispness.

d) Packing the Jars: Pack the sterilized jars tightly with the prepared produce, leaving some headspace at the top. Add your chosen spices and herbs (add sweeteners at this stage if desired). Cover the produce with the prepared brine, ensuring everything is fully submerged.

e) Sealing and Storing: Wipe the rims of the jars with a clean towel and tightly seal the jars with sterilized lids. Store the jars in a cool, dark place for about a week to allow the flavors to meld. Once opened, store any remaining pickles in the refrigerator.

3. Quick Pickling Method:

If you don't want to wait for a week, quick pickling offers a faster alternative. The steps involved in quick pickling are quite similar, with one key difference:

a) Heat Treatment: After packing the jars with produce and spices, bring the vinegar, water, salt, sweeteners, and any desired additional spices to a simmer in a saucepan. Remove it from heat and pour this hot liquid over the produce in the jars. Proceed to seal and store as per the traditional method.

Quick pickles are ready to eat within 24 hours, although flavors will continue to develop with longer storage.

4. Variations and Flavored Combinations:

The beauty of pickling lies in its endless possibilities. You can experiment with various fruits, such as strawberries, peaches, pears, grapes, pineapple, or even watermelon rinds. Tread into the realm of fusion cuisine by adding additional flavors like star anise, lemongrass, jalapenos, or even a touch of alcohol like gin or whiskey. The only limit is your culinary imagination!

In conclusion, pickling is not only a fantastic preservation method but also a delightful way to elevate the flavor profile of your favorite fruits and vegetables. Whether you choose to follow the traditional method or opt for the quick pickling technique, there is no denying the allure of tangy, crisp, and versatile pickled produce. So roll up your sleeves, gather your ingredients, and embark on a pickling adventure that will undoubtedly tantalize the tastebuds and impress your taste testers.

13

- The examples and recipes of dishes that use pickled fruits and vegetables in Africa

Africa has a rich culinary heritage that extends far beyond popular dishes like jollof rice or injera. One of the lesser-known but equally delicious traditions in African cuisine is the use of pickled fruits and vegetables in various traditional recipes. Pickling is a preservation method that has been used for centuries to extend the shelf life of perishable produce, and African cooks have perfected the art of pickling to create unique and flavorful dishes.

In West Africa, pickled vegetables are often used as a side dish or condiment to complement main dishes. One popular example is kpasi, a Nigerian pickled cabbage. To make kpasi, thinly sliced cabbage is fermented with a mixture of salt, Cameroon pepper, garlic, and onions. The result is a tangy and spicy pickle that adds a refreshing element to meals.

Another well-known West African accompaniment is atchara, a pickled vegetable relish that originated in the Philippines and was adapted by Cape Verdean immigrants in Senegal. Atchara is made by combining pickled green papaya, carrots, bell peppers, and onions with vinegar, sugar, and spices like ginger and garlic. It is often served as a condiment alongside grilled meats or seafood, providing a burst of zesty and slightly sweet flavors.

In East Africa, a popular pickled vegetable is rugula, which is made from a variety of leafy greens that have been fermented in a blend of water, salt, and spices. Rugula is commonly used in Tanzanian and Kenyan cuisine, where it is served as a side dish to accompany traditional staples such as ugali or chapati. This tangy and slightly bitter pickle adds a distinctive element to meals and enhances the overall flavor profile.

Moving down to Southern Africa, a classic pickling recipe comes from South Africa: chakalaka pickles. Chakalaka, a spicy vegetable relish, is added to jars and left to pickle, resulting in a delicious blend of flavors. The pickled vegetables, including carrots, cauliflower, green beans, and baby corn, soak up the fiery goodness of the chakalaka spice mix, creating a perfect combination of heat and tang.

Pickled fruits also play a role in African cuisine, particularly in the preparation of chutneys and sweet relishes. In Morocco, for example, preserved lemons are a staple in many traditional dishes. These lemons are preserved in a mixture of salt and their own juices, resulting in a distinctive tanginess that adds depth to tagines and couscous dishes. Similarly, in Egypt, pickled mango is widely enjoyed as a unique snack. Sliced green mangoes are pickled with a combination of vinegar, sugar, salt, and spices, resulting in a taste that is simultaneously sweet, tangy, savory, and spicy.

These examples merely scratch the surface of the variety of pickled fruits and vegetables found in African cuisine. From Senegal to South Africa, each region has its own unique specialty, resulting in a diverse array of pickled delicacies that add flavor and character to meals. So, next time you indulge in African cuisine, be sure to explore the delectable world of pickled fruits and vegetables and experience the culinary delights it has to offer.

Chapter 2: Fermented Cereals and Grains-The origin and distribution of fermented cereals and grains in Africa

Fermented cereals and grains have been an integral part of African diets for centuries. This chapter focuses on exploring the origin and distribution of fermented cereals and grains in Africa. Fermentation of these staple food sources has not only played a significant role in enhancing flavor and taste but also in improving nutritional value and digestibility. This chapter aims to shed light on the historical and cultural aspects of fermented cereals and grains in Africa.

1. Historical context:

1.1 Ancient origins: Fermentation of cereals and grains can be traced back to ancient civilizations in Africa. There is evidence of brewing beer, for instance, in Ancient Egypt dating back thousands of years. The use of fermented cereals and grains in daily food practices had a profound impact on the development of early African societies.

1.2 Indigenous knowledge: Indigenous African knowledge systems have contributed immensely to the art of fermentation. Traditional techniques and practices have been passed down through generations, shaping the diverse fermented food cultures found in different regions of Africa.

2. Distribution of fermented cereals and grains:

2.1 Eastern Africa: In Eastern Africa, sorghum and millet are commonly fermented to produce traditional alcoholic beverages such as chang'aa and tukawiri in Kenya, and togwa in Tanzania. Ugali, a popular porridge made from maize flour, is also sometimes fermented in this region.

2.2 Western Africa: Fermented cereals and grains form the foundation of many traditional dishes in West Africa. In Nigeria, for example, the fermentation of cassava gives rise to garri, a popular staple food. Other examples include lafun (fermented cassava flour) in Ghana and fufu (fermented cassava and plantain dough) in Liberia.

2.3 Central Africa: Cassava plays a crucial role in the fermented food culture of Central Africa. In the Democratic Republic of Congo, cassava is fermented to produce chikwange, while mabonde, kasaba, and chikwenga are fermented cassava dishes enjoyed in other Central African countries.

2.4 Southern Africa: Sorghum plays a significant role in the fermented food culture of Southern Africa. Maheu, a fermented maize drink, is popular in countries like Zimbabwe and Malawi. South Africa also has its unique fermented food traditions, such as umqombothi, a traditional beer made from sorghum and maize.

3. Nutritional benefits and health implications:

3.1 Improved digestibility: Fermentation breaks down complex carbohydrates present in cereals and grains, making them more easily digestible. This improves nutrient absorption and reduces the risk of digestive disorders.

3.2 Increased nutrient bioavailability: Fermentation enhances the bioavailability of nutrients such as iron, calcium, and zinc, making them more accessible to the body. This is particularly important in addressing micronutrient deficiencies prevalent in many African communities.

3.3 Probiotic potential: Fermented cereals and grains are a rich source of beneficial microorganisms that promote gut health and boost the immune system. These probiotic effects have been associated with improved overall health and wellbeing.

———◦———

FERMENTED CEREALS AND grains have a long-standing history in African food cultures, representing an essential part of traditional diets. The distribution of fermented cereals and grains across various regions of Africa highlights the diverse nature of African cuisine. Beyond being a culinary tradition, fermentation offers numerous nutritional benefits and contributes to overall health and wellbeing. Preserving and promoting the traditional methods of fermentation are vital for safeguarding African culinary heritage and ensuring sustainable food systems.

- The ingredients and methods of making fermented cereals and grains in different ways

Fermentation has been an integral part of human civilization for thousands of years. It is a process that involves the breakdown of organic materials by microorganisms such as bacteria or yeast. This process not only helps enhance the flavor, aroma, and texture of our food but also contributes to its nutritional value. One of the most fascinating applications of fermentation is in the preparation of fermented cereals and grains, which are widely consumed around the world. Let's explore the various ingredients and methods used in making fermented cereals and grains in different ways.

1. Souring agents:

Fermentation requires the presence of microorganisms that can break down the starches and sugars in cereals and grains into simpler compounds. One of the primary ways to achieve this is by using souring agents such as lactic acid bacteria or wild yeast. These agents help lower the pH of the mixture, creating an ideal environment for beneficial bacteria to thrive.

2. Water:

Water is a crucial component in the fermentation process. It helps facilitate the activation of enzymes present in the cereal or grain, creating the necessary conditions for fermentation to occur. The amount of water used can vary depending on the type of fermented product being made.

3. Cereal or grain:

The choice of cereal or grain used can vary depending on regional preferences and availability. Some commonly used cereals and grains include rice, millet, maize, wheat, and barley. Each grain has a unique nutrient profile and flavor, resulting in distinct flavors in the final product.

4. Soaking:

Before the fermentation process, the cereals or grains need to be properly soaked. Soaking helps break down the antinutrients present in the cereals, including phytic acid and enzyme inhibitors that can interfere with nutrient absorption. It also softens the grains, making them easier to cook and ferment.

5. Bruising or milling:

In some traditional fermentation processes, such as for the production of fermented rice or corn, the cereals or grains are lightly bruised or milled. This step helps activate enzymes within the grain and enhances the fermentation process. In modern industrial settings, milling is sometimes replaced with the addition of enzymes to achieve the same effect.

6. Fermentation vessels:

The choice of fermentation vessel can impact the flavor and texture of the final product. Traditional methods often use clay pots, wooden barrels, or banana leaves to ferment cereals and grains. These vessels provide a natural and porous environment, allowing the exchange of gases while maintaining a consistent temperature. In contrast, modern methods may utilize stainless steel tanks or airtight containers that offer more control over the fermentation process.

7. Fermentation time and temperature:

The duration and temperature of fermentation play a critical role in determining the flavor and nutritional characteristics of fermented cereals and grains. Traditionally, fermentation took place at ambient temperatures for extended periods, ranging from a few days to several months. Nowadays, temperature-controlled environments are employed to ensure consistency and minimize the risk of unwanted microbial contamination.

8. Post-fermentation processing:

After fermentation, the cereals and grains may undergo additional processing steps to improve their shelf life, taste, or texture. These can include drying, steaming, roasting, or further cooking. These post-fermentation procedures may vary depending on the desired final product.

In conclusion, the art of fermenting cereals and grains is a time-honored tradition that continues to be practiced in various ways across different cultures. As we explore the diverse flavors and nutritional benefits of fermented foods, it is important to appreciate the ingredients and methods that contribute to their unique properties. Experimentation with different ingredients and fermentation techniques allows us to discover an array of delicious and wholesome fermented cereals and grains, enriching our culinary experiences.

- The examples and recipes of dishes that use fermented cereals and grains in Africa

Fermented cereals and grains are widely used in African cuisine, offering a unique and distinctive flavor to various dishes. These fermented products not only enhance the taste but also increase the nutritional value of the foods. Let's explore some fascinating examples and recipes of dishes that use fermented cereals and grains across different regions in Africa.

1. Injera (Ethiopia and Eritrea):

Injera, a traditional Ethiopian and Eritrean flatbread, is widely consumed throughout these countries. It is made by fermenting teff, a nutritious and gluten-free grain, for several days. The resulting batter is then cooked into large, sourdough-like crepes that are often used as a utensil to scoop stews and other dishes.

Recipe: To make injera, start by mixing equal parts teff flour and water. Allow the mixture to ferment for about three days, covered and undisturbed, at room temperature. After fermentation, a slightly tangy and bubbly batter is obtained. Heat a non-stick skillet over medium heat and pour a ladle of batter in a circular motion. Cook for 2-3 minutes until the edges detach and the bottom is cooked. Injera is usually served rolled up or folded.

2. Ogiri (Nigeria):

Ogiri is a traditional fermented condiment commonly used in Nigerian cuisine. It is made by fermenting a combination of legumes, cereals, and oilseeds. One of the primary ingredients in ogiri is dawadawa, which comes from the seeds of the African locust bean tree. Ogiri adds a distinct umami flavor to soups, stews, and sauces.

Recipe: Making ogiri is a lengthy process that involves fermenting and processing several ingredients. Start by boiling the African locust bean seeds until they are soft, typically for about four hours. Once cooled, mash the seeds into a paste and mix them with salt. Transfer the mixture to a container and ferment it for several days. It will become a dark, flavorful condiment with a pungent smell. Use ogiri sparingly in your soups and stews to enhance the taste.

3. Kenkey (Ghana):

Kenkey is a staple food in Ghana, prepared from fermented maize or cornmeal. It is a popular dish and often eaten with fried fish, stewed vegetables, or pepper sauce. The fermentation process gives the dish a sour taste and a soft, moist texture.

Recipe: To make kenkey, start by soaking dry-milled maize overnight. The soaked maize is then wet-milled to obtain a smoother consistency. The wet flour is left to ferment for 2-3 days, covered to create the right conditions. After fermentation, shape the fermented dough into cylindrical portions wrapped in banana leaves or corn husks. Steam the wrapped dough for several hours until cooked. Serve kenkey as a main dish or as a side with various sauces.

4. Togbei (Benin):

Togbei is a fermented corn drink enjoyed in Benin, offering a refreshing and slightly sour taste. It is commonly consumed during festive occasions or as a traditional breakfast. Togbei is made by fermenting soaked and crushed corn kernels for two to three days, resulting in a delicious beverage that is rich in essential nutrients.

Recipe: Prepare togbei by soaking whole dried corn kernels in water for about 24 hours until they soften. Once softened, remove the corn's hulls and grind the corn using a mill or grinder. Add water to the corn paste and cover it for two to three days, allowing fermentation to take place. After fermentation, strain the liquid to separate the corn solids, and chill the beverage before serving.

These are just a few captivating examples and recipes showcasing how fermented cereals and grains are incorporated into African cuisine. The fermentation process not only brings unique flavors but also creates nutritious and culturally significant food items that have been enjoyed for generations.

Chapter 3: Fermented Tubers and Roots- The origin and distribution of fermented tubers and roots in Africa

Fermentation has long been a traditional method of food preservation and processing in many cultures around the world. In Africa, fermented tubers and roots hold a significant place in the culinary traditions of various ethnic groups. This chapter aims to explore the origin and distribution of fermented tubers and roots in Africa, shedding light on their historical and cultural significance.

History and Origins:

The fermentation of tubers and roots in Africa has its roots in ancient times, dating back thousands of years. Archaeological evidence reveals that early African civilizations, such as the ancient Egyptians, Ethiopians, and Nubians, had already mastered the art of fermenting tubers and roots.

The Nile River Valley was a hub of agricultural activity, with ancient civilizations growing and utilizing a wide range of tubers and roots. Notably, the Egyptians cultivated lotus roots, cattail tubers, and papyrus stems, all of which were later incorporated into various fermented dishes.

As centuries passed, the knowledge and techniques of fermenting tubers and roots spread across the African continent through trade routes, cultural exchanges, and migrations. The extensive diversity of African tubers and roots enabled local communities to develop unique methods and recipes for fermentation, leading to a rich culinary heritage that remains vibrant in present times.

Distribution:

The distribution of fermented tubers and roots in Africa is extensive, reflecting the continent's diverse ecosystems and cultural variations. Each region has its own set of tubers and roots that are commonly fermented and incorporated into local cuisines.

In West Africa, tubers like yam, cassava, and cocoyam are widely used in fermentation processes. Fermented cassava, known as gari, is a staple food in Nigeria and Ghana, while fermented yam products, such as foo-foo and amala, are famous in countries like Nigeria, Ghana, and Benin.

Moving towards Central Africa, tubers like African breadfruit, taro, and sweet potato take center stage. For example, fermented taro leaves, known as pondu, are a popular Congolese delicacy, while fermented sweet potato, known as otipuis, is a staple food in Cameroon.

In Eastern Africa, root crops like arrowroot, cassava, and sweet potatoes dominate fermentation practices. The Maasai of Kenya and Tanzania ferment arrowroot into a traditional porridge called busaa. Additionally, ugali, a staple food made from fermented cassava or maize, is commonly consumed by many East African communities.

Southern Africa exhibits a wide range of fermented tuber and root products as well. Fermented wild potatoes, known as maqatha, are traditionally made by the San people. Cassava's fermentation is also widespread, especially in countries like Zambia and Malawi, where products like chikanda, a fermented cassava cake, are highly regarded.

⟿ ❧ ⟾

THE ORIGIN AND DISTRIBUTION of fermented tubers and roots in Africa reveal a deep-rooted connection between traditional cuisines, regional diversity, and ancestral practices. The diverse range of tubers and roots available across the continent has nurtured a plethora of fermentation techniques and recipes that continue to be passed down through generations. Understanding the cultural and historical significance of fermented tubers and roots in Africa allows for a deeper appreciation of the continent's rich culinary heritage.

- The ingredients and methods of making fermented tubers and roots in different ways

Fermented tubers and roots have been a part of traditional diets in many cultures around the world for centuries. These nutrient-rich foods provide important sources of carbohydrates, vitamins, minerals, and microbiota to support gut health. In this article, we will explore various ingredients and methods used for fermenting tubers and roots.

1. Ingredients:

a. Tubers and roots: Some commonly used ones include yams, sweet potatoes, cassava, taro, ginger, turmeric, beets, and carrots. These tubers and roots contain starches and sugars that serve as food for the fermenting microorganisms.

b. Starter culture: Lactic acid bacteria present naturally on the vegetables, specifically on the surface, are usually sufficient to initiate fermentation. However, starters can be supplemented to ensure a quick and consistent fermentation process. Examples of starter cultures are whey, sauerkraut juice, or brines from previously fermented vegetables.

c. Salt: Salt acts as a natural preservative while preventing the growth of undesirable bacteria. It is essential for balancing the fermentation process and creating favorable conditions for beneficial bacteria.

d. Herbs and spices: Ingredients like garlic, chili peppers, dill, black pepper, or bay leaves can be added for flavor and aroma.

2. Methods:

a. Basic lacto-fermentation: This method is easiest and commonly used for tubers and roots. Start by thinly slicing or grating the tubers/roots. Then, sprinkle salt over them and let them sit for around 30 minutes. The salt helps draw out moisture and initiates the fermentation process. Pack the tubers/roots tightly into a clean glass jar and press them down firmly. The liquid released from the salted vegetables should cover them completely. Place a weight or fermentation disk on top to keep them submerged. Close the jar loosely to allow the carbon dioxide produced during fermentation to escape. Let it ferment at room temperature for at least 5-7 days, or until the desired flavor and texture are achieved. Check on it daily to ensure that the vegetables are fully submerged.

b. Two-stage fermentation: This method involves a two-step fermentation process. Begin as in the basic lacto-fermentation process, but instead of pressing the vegetables into a jar, allow them to ferment in an open container for a day or two. This step encourages anaerobic fermentation, with carbon dioxide being released. After this initial fermentation, transfer the vegetables to a clean, airtight jar, packing them tightly and submerging them under their own liquid or brine. Seal the jar and allow it to ferment for an additional period, typically 5-7 days, or longer if preferred.

3. Additional considerations:

a. Temperature: Lacto-fermentation occurs best within a temperature range of 18-24°C (64-75°F). Slower fermentation at lower temperatures will produce a tangier flavor, while a warmer environment speeds up the process.

b. Hygiene: Ensure all equipment used for fermentation is clean to avoid contamination from unwanted bacteria or molds.

c. Taste-testing: Taste the ferment periodically to determine when it reaches the desired flavor. If it becomes too sour, fermentation can be stopped by transferring to the refrigerator, which will slow down the fermentation process.

- The examples and recipes of dishes that use fermented tubers and roots in Africa

In Africa, there is a long-standing tradition of fermenting tubers and roots to create a variety of delicious and nutritious dishes. Fermentation not only enhances the flavor of these ingredients but also increases their nutritional value by making the vitamins and minerals they contain more bioavailable. Let's dive into some examples and recipes of dishes that showcase the incredible versatility and health benefits of fermented tubers and roots in African cuisine.

1. Ugba/Ukpaka (Fermented Oil Bean)

Ugba, also known as Ukpaka, is a popular fermented oil bean dish originating from the Igbo people of Nigeria. It is made by fermenting oil bean seeds, which come from the Velvet Tamarind tree. To prepare Ugba, the oil bean seeds are soaked in water for a couple of days until they soften and naturally ferment. After fermentation, the beans are washed, boiled, and combined with spices, vegetables, and sometimes fish or meat. The resulting delicacy is packed with umami and enjoyed with various Nigerian staples like pounded yam or garri (cassava flakes).

2. Injera (Ethiopian Fermented Flatbread)

Injera is a well-known Ethiopian fermented flatbread made primarily from teff flour. Teff is a tiny grain found in Ethiopia and is fermented for several days before being made into batter. The batter is then cooked into a large, spongy bread with a distinct sour taste and bubbly texture. Injera is a staple in Ethiopian cuisine, serving as not only a bread but also a utensil. It is commonly used to scoop up stews and sautéed vegetables, adding a tangy element to the overall meal.

3. Kivunde (Fermented Cassava Porridge)

Kivunde is a traditional dish from the Kikuyu and Embu people of Kenya, made by fermenting cassava to create porridge. Cassava, also known as yuca, is grated and soaked in water for a few days. During this time, natural fermentation takes place. After fermentation, the cassava pulp is pressed to extract excess liquid, then cooked to make a fluffy porridge. Kivunde is often paired with a meat-based stew or flavored with various spices and served as a standalone meal.

4. Banku (Ghanaian Fermented Corn and Cassava Dumplings)

Banku is a traditional fermented dish from Ghana made by combining corn and cassava dough. To make banku, white cornmeal and cassava flour are mixed together with water and left to ferment for a few days or until it develops a slightly sour taste. The fermented batter is then mixed, molded into balls, and boiled. Banku is typically served with okra soup, groundnut soup, or grilled fish, providing a fantastic textural contrast and unique flavor profile.

5. Kimchi (South African Fermented Cabbage)

Kimchi may be traditionally associated with Korean cuisine, but South Africa has its own version of this delicious fermented vegetable dish. South African kimchi typically consists of cabbage, carrots, radishes, onions, garlic, and chillies, all fermented together in a brine solution. The mixture is left to ferment for a couple of weeks, allowing the flavors to develop and intensify. South African kimchi adds vibrancy and spiciness to a variety of dishes, including stews, grains, and sandwiches.

These are just a few examples of the rich culinary heritage that stems from fermenting tubers and roots in various African cultures. The incredible range of flavors, textures, and health benefits offered by fermented dishes makes them staples in African households. So, the next time you're looking for some culinary inspiration, consider exploring these delightful fermented tuber and root-based recipes from Africa.

Chapter 4: Fermented Milk and Dairy- The origin and distribution of fermented milk and dairy in Africa

Fermented milk and dairy have been an integral part of African cuisine and culture for centuries. These unique products are not only nutritious but also play a vital role in preserving milk and extending its shelf life, especially in regions where access to refrigeration is limited. This chapter focuses on the origin and distribution of fermented milk and dairy in Africa, shedding light on the rich history and diverse practices associated with these products.

1. Historical Perspectives:

The consumption of fermented milk and dairy in Africa can be traced back to ancient times. Native communities across the continent, like the Maasai in East Africa and the Fulani in West Africa, have long recognized the benefits of fermenting milk. Archaeological findings have provided evidence of fermented milk being consumed thousands of years ago, highlighting its importance in African food culture.

2. Traditional Fermentation Techniques:

Various traditional fermentation techniques are employed in Africa to ferment milk and dairy products. One popular method involves the use of starter cultures derived from naturally occurring lactic acid bacteria, which are responsible for the fermentation process. These starter cultures are often obtained from previous batches of fermented milk or through spontaneous fermentation. Additionally, specific herbs or plants may be added to enhance the flavor and aroma of the final product.

3. Regional Variations and Products:

Africa is an incredibly diverse continent, and this diversity is reflected in its fermented milk and dairy products. Different regions have their own unique variations and preparations of these products. For instance, in East Africa, fermented milk is known as "mursik" among the Kalenjin people of Kenya and takes the form of a thick, sour milk traditionally stored in animal hide. In West

Africa, "nunu" is a popular fermented milk product made by the Fulani people using calabashes for fermentation.

4. Health Benefits and Nutritional Value:

Fermented milk and dairy are not only rich in essential nutrients like calcium, proteins, and vitamins, but also harbor probiotic bacteria, which promote gut health and strengthen the immune system. These products are not just a staple in the African diet but also help combat malnutrition, a prevalent issue in many parts of the continent.

5. Challenges and Future Perspectives:

Despite the significance of fermented milk and dairy in African cuisine, there are challenges to its widespread production and consumption. Factors such as limited access to education, scarce resources, and a lack of proper infrastructures for production pose barriers to the growth of the industry. However, with increased awareness and support, there is a promising future for the revival and development of fermented milk and dairy in Africa.

THE ORIGIN AND DISTRIBUTION of fermented milk and dairy in Africa have deep roots in the continent's history and culture. These products not only offer health benefits but also contribute to food security by prolonging the shelf life of milk. By embracing and preserving their traditional practices while also exploring new innovations, African communities can ensure the continued availability and appreciation of these precious fermented products for generations to come.

- The ingredients and methods of making fermented milk and dairy in different ways

Making fermented milk and dairy products is a time-honored tradition that dates back centuries. The process involves using live bacteria cultures to break down the lactose in the milk and convert it into lactic acid. This fermentation not only preserves the milk, but also imparts a unique tangy flavor and texture to the final product.

There are several methods for making fermented milk and dairy, each lending itself to different types of products. Let's explore some of these methods and the ingredients involved.

1. Yogurt:

Yogurt is perhaps the most famous form of fermented milk. It is made by heating milk, usually cow's milk, to a certain temperature to kill off any undesired bacteria and create an ideal environment for starter cultures to thrive. These starter cultures contain lactic acid bacteria, such as Lactobacillus bulgaricus and Streptococcus thermophilus, which are added to the milk. After being incubated at a specific temperature for a set period, the natural bacteria in these cultures convert the lactose in the milk into lactic acid, resulting in a creamy, tangy yogurt.

2. Kefir:

Kefir is another popular fermented milk product that originates from the Caucasus region. It is made using kefir grains, which are small lumpy structures containing bacteria and yeast. To make kefir, these grains are introduced to milk, usually cow's or goat's milk. The milk is then left to ferment for around 24 hours at room temperature. The bacteria and yeast present in the kefir grains consume the lactose and produce various acids, alcohol, and carbon dioxide, resulting in a fizzy, slightly alcoholic beverage. Kefir is known for its probiotic qualities and has a tart, tangy flavor.

3. Cheese:

Cheese can also be considered a form of fermented dairy, as the primary ingredient, milk, needs to undergo fermentation to transform into cheese. The use of starter cultures, like Lactococcus lactis, Lactobacillus helveticus, and various strains of mold or fungi like Penicillium roqueforti, play a crucial role in the fermentation process. These cultures give cheese its characteristic flavor, texture, and aroma. The process of cheese making involves several steps, including adding starter cultures and rennet (an enzyme that curdles the milk), curdling, cutting, heating, and pressing. Depending on the type of cheese desired, the process and ingredients can vary significantly.

4. Buttermilk:

Traditionally, buttermilk was the byproduct of churning butter from cream. Nowadays, it is often made by fermenting milk with specific bacteria cultures. The bacteria, such as Lactococcus lactis and Leuconostoc mesenteroides, consume the lactose in the milk and produce lactic acid, giving buttermilk its tangy taste. Buttermilk can be used in baking, cooking, or enjoyed as a refreshing drink.

5. Labneh:

Labneh, also known as strained yogurt or yogurt cheese, is made by further fermenting yogurt and removing its whey. The process involves placing yogurt in a cheesecloth or muslin bag and allowing the whey to drain off slowly over a period of time, usually overnight. This results in a thick, creamy spreadable cheese with a tangy flavor. Labneh is commonly enjoyed as a dip, spread on bread or used as a base for creamy sauces.

In conclusion, the process of making fermented milk and dairy products involves the use of specific bacteria cultures or grains, along with different techniques for fermentation and subsequent processing. The resulting products, such as yogurt, kefir, cheese, buttermilk, and labneh, have unique characteristics and flavors that make them beloved staples in different cultures around the world.

- The examples and recipes of dishes that use fermented milk and dairy in Africa

Fermented milk and dairy play a significant role in African cuisine, adding rich flavors and diverse textures to various dishes. Here, we explore some intriguing examples and provide delicious recipes that highlight the exquisite use of fermented milk and dairy in Africa.

1. Mala (Kenya):

Mala, a popular fermented milk beverage in Kenya, is made from fresh whole milk left to ferment naturally overnight. The addition of a live starter culture further enhances its tangy taste and thick consistency. To prepare Mala, simply cover a bowl of whole milk and let it naturally ferment for at least 8 hours or overnight. Serve it chilled with meals or enjoy it on its own for a refreshing experience.

2. Amasi (South Africa):

Amasi, also known as maas or Mageu, is a traditional fermented milk widely consumed in South Africa. It has a custard-like texture with a pleasantly sour taste. To make Amasi, start by heating milk until it reaches a boil. Allow it to cool until the temperature is lukewarm (around 40-45°C). Add a small amount of previously fermented milk or a commercial starter culture, and leave the mixture undisturbed in a warm place for 12-24 hours. Once fermented, refrigerate the Amasi until thickened and chilled. Serve it as a beverage or use it as an ingredient in various dishes such as milktart or pap (maize porridge).

3. Ayib (Ethiopia):

Ayib is a delicious Ethiopian cottage cheese made from fermented milk known as Ersho. To prepare Ayib, start by bringing milk to a boil, then allow it to cool to lukewarm temperature (about 45°C). Add a teaspoon of previously prepared Ayib or a starter culture, then place the mixture in a warm place, undisturbed, for 6-12 hours. Once the milk has formed a solid curd, line a strainer with cheese cloth and pour the curdled milk into it. Let it drain for 2-3 hours, then refrigerate the resulting cottage cheese. Ayib can be enjoyed as a condiment, crumbled on dishes, or used as a filling in various Ethiopian recipes like the popular injera flatbread.

4. Zabady (Egypt):

Zabady is a thick, tangy, and slightly fermented milk commonly served in Egyptian households and enjoyed throughout the Middle East. You can make your own zabady by combining equal parts yogurt and laban (cultured buttermilk); let the mixture ferment for 12-24 hours until thickened. The result is a delectable, spoonable creamy treat that can be enjoyed as a refreshing beverage or as a component in savory dishes.

These are just a few examples of dishes that make wonderful use of fermented milk and dairy in African cuisine. Whether you prefer a tangy beverage, a creamy cottage cheese, or a refreshing addition to your recipes, exploring the world of fermented milk and dairy in African food will open a whole new dimension of flavors and textures to savor and enjoy.

Chapter 5: Fermented Meat and Fish- The origin and distribution of fermented meat and fish in Africa

Fermented meat and fish have been an integral part of African culinary traditions for centuries. These traditional preservation techniques have allowed local communities to prolong the shelf life of meat and fish, making them indispensable in regions lacking refrigeration. In this chapter, we delve into the origin, techniques, and distribution of fermented meat and fish in Africa, highlighting the cultural significance and unique flavors associated with these fermented delicacies.

1. The Origins of Fermentation in Africa:

Fermentation as a method of food preservation can be traced back to ancient times, where the indigenous African population came up with innovative ways to preserve their food in the absence of modern technology. This section will explore the historical evidence of fermented meat and fish found in archaeological sites, demonstrating that these preservation techniques have been a part of African culinary practices for several millennia.

2. Techniques of Fermentation:

In this section, we examine the various techniques used in fermenting meat and fish across different African regions. From drying and salting to smoking and marinating, each technique carries unique cultural and regional peculiarities. We explore different fermentation agents like salt, spices, and microorganisms, shedding light on the complex process of transforming raw meat and fish into savory, preserved products.

3. Regional Variations and Flavor Profiles:

Africa is a vast continent with diverse ethnicities and culinary traditions. In this section, we delve into the regional variations of fermented meat and fish preparations. From the Moroccan delicacy "Khlea" to the Nigerian "Kilishi" and "Akokono" of Ghana, we unravel the rich tapestry of flavors and textures that make each region's fermented meat and fish unique. Through ethnographic studies and interviews with local culinary experts, we explore how regional ingredients, spices, and cultural preferences shape the taste and characteristics of these products.

4. Health Benefits and Nutritional Value:

Apart from being an essential preservation method, fermented meat and fish also offer a myriad of health benefits. In this section, we investigate the nutritional values of these fermented delicacies. Rich in proteins, vitamins, and minerals, we highlight how fermented meat and fish can contribute to a balanced diet, even in resource-limited regions. Additionally, we explore the potential probiotic effects of the microorganisms involved in the fermentation process.

5. Commercialization and Challenges:

Although fermented meat and fish hold cultural and historical significance, they face numerous challenges in modern times. This section examines the impact of commercialization and globalization on traditional fermentation methods, outlining both positive and negative consequences. Moreover, we investigate the hurdles faced in regulating commercial production, ensuring food safety, and maintaining the authenticity and traditional values of fermented meat and fish.

FERMENTED MEAT AND fish are not only essential for sustenance but also represent an integral part of African culinary heritage. By exploring their origins, techniques, regional variations, and health benefits, we shed light on the diverse cultural nuances associated with these fermented delicacies. Moreover, we address the challenges and opportunities faced in their commercialization, highlighting the importance of preserving and promoting these traditional practices for future generations to savor and appreciate.

- The ingredients and methods of making fermented meat and fish in different ways

Fermented meat and fish have long been a part of various cuisines around the world. The process of fermentation not only imparts unique flavors and textures to these ingredients but also aids in their preservation, allowing people to enjoy them well beyond their natural shelf life. In this article, we will explore the ingredients and methods involved in making fermented meat and fish in different ways.

The Ingredients:

1. Meat or Fish:

The choice of the main ingredient depends on the desired outcome. For fermented meat, popular options include beef, pork, and poultry. Similarly, for fermented fish, options like anchovies, mackerel, and herrings are commonly used due to their high-fat content which aids in the fermentation process.

2. Salt:

Salt plays a crucial role in fermentation as it inhibits the growth of harmful bacteria while supporting the growth of beneficial ones. Different recipes call for varying amounts of salt based on personal preferences and traditional practices.

3. Spices and Herbs:

Depending on the desired flavors, spices and herbs can be added to the fermentation process. Examples include coriander, pepper, chili, and various herbs like thyme or rosemary. These additions infuse the meat or fish with a unique taste profile.

4. Starter Cultures:

In some cases, specific starter cultures are added to the meat or fish to kick-start the fermentation process. These cultures contain beneficial bacteria or yeasts that aid in breaking down the proteins and fats, leading to a favorable fermentation outcome.

The Methods:

1. Dry Aging:

One popular method for fermenting meat involves dry aging. In this process, meat is placed in a controlled environment with controlled temperature and humidity conditions. The naturally present bacteria on the meat's surface initiate the fermentation process over time, leading to changes in flavor, tenderness, and overall quality of the meat.

2. Salt Curing:

Salt curing is extensively used for fermenting fish. The fish is coated with salt, enhancing the flavors and drawing out moisture from the fish. The salt helps preserve the fish while encouraging fermentation. This method is widely employed in preparing delicacies like salted fish, salted herrings, and salted roe.

3. Fermentation in Brine:

Brine fermentation is a method where the meat or fish is immersed in a saltwater solution (brine). This environment encourages the growth of beneficial bacteria while preventing the development of harmful pathogens. The fermentation process can take several weeks to months, during which flavors develop, acidity increases, and the texture changes.

4. Starter Culture Fermentation:

To ensure precise control over the fermentation process, starter cultures can be added to the meat or fish. These cultures accelerate fermentation by introducing specific strains of bacteria or yeasts. The use of starter cultures allows for greater consistency of the final product, making it popular in commercial food production.

In conclusion, fermented meat and fish are culinary delights that showcase the art of ancient preservation techniques. The ingredients, including choice of meat or fish, salt, spices, and herbs, need to be carefully selected to achieve desired flavors. The methods of fermentation, such as dry aging, salt curing, fermentation in brine, or utilizing starter cultures, contribute to unique textures and tastes. Whether you are indulging in Korean kimchi or Scandinavian gravlax, the diverse world of fermented meats and fish promises a tantalizing journey to our taste buds.

- The examples and recipes of dishes that use fermented meat and fish in Africa

Fermented meat and fish play significant roles in African cuisine, not only enhancing the flavor of dishes but also serving as a means of food preservation. These practices have been part of traditional African cooking for centuries and are celebrated for their unique taste and cultural significance. Let's delve into some intriguing examples and mouthwatering recipes that showcase the diverse use of fermented meat and fish in Africa.

1. Pemba- This fermented meat dish hails from Mozambique and is prepared by marinating beef or pork ribs in a puree of onions, garlic, hot peppers, and traditional spices. The mixture is then left to ferment for several days, allowing the flavors to meld and the meat to tenderize. The result is a succulent and highly spicy dish that pairs well with rice or cornmeal.

2. Kelewele- Originating from Ghana, kelewele is a scrumptious street food made by fermenting plantains and then frying them. The ripe plantains are typically diced into chunks and combined with a mixture of grated ginger, chili peppers, cloves, and salt. After a day of fermentation, the plantains are fried until golden brown, creating a flavorful and slightly tangy snack.

3. Shirako- In East Africa, especially in countries like Kenya and Tanzania, the fermented fish dish called shirako is revered. It involves preserving small freshwater fish, such as Nile perch or tilapia, by salting and sun-drying them. Once dried, these fish are typically pounded into a fine powder and incorporated into various stews and soups, imparting a rich umami flavor.

4. Isi Ewu- A popular traditional Igbo dish from Nigeria, isi ewu showcases the African love for fermented meats. It revolves around a goat head that is cleaned, roasted, and marinated in a flavorful blend of onions, utazi leaves, traditional powder spices, and a little locust bean seasoning for up to 24 hours. The meat is then cooked until tender, creating a delicious dish often served alongside palm wine or chilled drinks.

5. Pounded Yams with Eru- Hailing from Cameroon, this fermented meat and fish dish utilizes eru leaves, which are fermented for days to develop a tangy flavor. The leaves are then cooked with smoked fish, crayfish, and palm oil. The resulting sauce is enjoyed with pounded yam, creating a hearty and deeply satisfying meal.

6. Maasai cuisine- The Maasai community in East Africa is known for incorporating fermented blood and milk in their diet. This mixture, called "yooko", is obtained by collecting fresh cow blood, adding milk, and sealing it in a large gourd to ferment for several hours. The fermented beverage is an important Maasai food source, providing vital nutrients and proteins.

These examples highlight the expansive diversity of fermented meat and fish dishes in Africa, showcasing the continent's unique culinary heritage. From Mozambique to Nigeria and Ghana to Cameroon, Africa's flavorful fermented dishes offer a tantalizing taste of tradition and culture.

Chapter 6: Injera- The origin and popularity of injera in Ethiopia and Eritrea

In this chapter, we will delve into the fascinating history and widespread popularity of injera, a traditional Ethiopian and Eritrean staple food. Injera, a fermented sourdough flatbread, has come to symbolize the unique gastronomic cultures of these two African nations. We will explore the origins of injera, understand the traditional techniques involved in its preparation, and uncover the reasons behind its significant influence and widespread fame.

1. Origins of Injera:

Historical evidence suggests that injera has been a part of Ethiopian and Eritrean cuisine for over a thousand years. The first mentions of injera can be found in ancient texts and religious scripts dating back to the 6th century. Various theories exist regarding the origins of injera, with some linking it to the Aksumite civilization and others associating it with the Ethiopian Queen of Sheba. However, it remains uncertain whether injera was brought to this region or developed locally.

2. Traditional Preparation Techniques:

To truly appreciate the cultural significance of injera, it is crucial to understand the traditional methods employed in its preparation. Traditionally, injera batter is made by fermenting a mixture of teff flour and water for several days. Teff, a highly nutritious grain indigenous to Ethiopia and Eritrea, is the backbone of genuine injera. The fermented batter undergoes a natural leavening process with the help of wild yeast present in the environment. The batter is then poured onto a hot clay griddle called a mitad and cooked, resulting in a spongy, pancake-like bread with a unique tart flavor.

3. Regional Variations and Accoutrements:

While the basic recipe for injera remains mostly unchanged, there are slight regional variations in terms of texture and taste. Injera prepared in the highlands of Ethiopia, for example, tends to be slightly sourer and lighter in color compared to the version popular in Eritrea. Additionally, injera made with a mix of grains, such as wheat or barley, are also found in certain regions. Injera's role as a staple food is evident in its accompaniments, which include a diverse array of stews, vegetables, and dips collectively known as 'wats'. The combination of injera and wats creates a complete and satisfying meal.

4. Cultural Impact and Popularity:

Injera plays a significant role in Ethiopian and Eritrean cultures, extending beyond its culinary applications. It is often central to social gatherings and significant ceremonies, where it is shared amongst family members and friends. The act of tearing a piece of injera and using it to scoop up bites of seasoned meat or vegetables is considered an important cultural practice, fostering communal dining and reinforcing social bonds. Furthermore, as Ethiopian and Eritrean diasporas have spread across the globe, so too has the popularity of injera. Today, an increasing number of restaurants catering to international audiences serve injera, leading to its mainstream recognition and adoption by a wider culinary audience.

***

INJERA, WITH ITS CENTURIES-old history and cultural significance, stands as an emblem of Ethiopian and Eritrean cuisine. Its traditional preparation techniques, regional variations, and role in fostering communal dining have ensured its popularity throughout the world. As we conclude this chapter, it becomes evident that injera's enduring appeal lies not only in its delicious flavor but also in its ability to reflect the rich traditions and vibrant heritage of Ethiopia and Eritrea.

- The ingredients and methods of making injera from fermented teff flour

Injera is a traditional Ethiopian flatbread that is not only a staple in Ethiopian cuisine but also a key component of their culture and tradition. Made from fermented teff flour, injera is not your average bread but instead boasts a unique flavor and spongy texture that perfectly complements the various stews and dishes it is commonly served with. The process of making injera involves a combination of specific ingredients and careful methods to ensure the perfect end result.

The first and most crucial ingredient for making injera is teff flour. Teff is a highly nutritious grain that is native to Ethiopia and is known for its small size and earthy flavor. Injera is traditionally made from the darker varieties of teff flour as they provide a richer taste and distinct color. Teff flour can be found at specialty stores or online. While it is entirely possible to make injera solely from teff flour, some recipes suggest using a combination of teff and all-purpose flour to achieve a lighter texture.

The second key ingredient in making injera is water. The water used in the fermentation process should be warm to aid in the activation of the fermenting agents. Filtered water is preferred to avoid any impurities that could potentially affect the fermentation process.

The next set of ingredients are crucial for the fermentation of the teff flour. Injera requires a starter or a culture to activate the fermentation process. Traditionally, a small amount of previous injera batter is mixed into the fresh teff flour and water mixture to provide the necessary lactic acid bacteria needed for fermentation. However, commercial yeast can also be used as a substitute for convenience. There are also specialized injera starter cultures available online or at specific African grocery stores.

Once the ingredients are assembled, the process of making injera begins with the fermentation of the teff flour and water mixture. To do this, the teff flour is combined with warm water in a large mixing bowl. The mixture should have a consistency similar to pancake batter. It is then covered with a clean kitchen towel and set aside at room temperature for at least 24 to 48 hours. During this time, the mixture is left to ferment, allowing the growth of lactic acid bacteria that contribute to the unique taste and texture of injera.

After the fermentation period, the batter will develop a sour smell and slightly bubbly appearance, indicating that it is ready for cooking. Before starting to cook the injera, the batter should be vigorously stirred to incorporate air and create additional bubbles.

To prepare the injera, a non-stick pan called a mitad or a large flat griddle can be used. The pan should be heated on medium-high heat. Once heated, a ladle or measuring cup is used to pour the batter onto the pan, starting in the center and moving outwards in a circular motion. The batter is spread thinly across the surface of the pan to create a large, round injera.

The injera is cooked solely on one side, without flipping it over. This means that the pan needs to retain a consistent temperature throughout the cooking process. It usually takes a few minutes for the injera to cook. When it is ready, it develops a distinct bubbly appearance and starts to pull away from the edges of the pan.

Once cooked, the injera is usually stacked on a plate in a warm place to keep it soft and pliable. Traditionally, it is served by placing various stews and dishes on top of a large injera, which is then torn into smaller pieces to be eaten by hand.

In conclusion, making injera from fermented teff flour requires a few essential ingredients and careful attention to detail. The process of fermentation brings out the unique taste and texture of injera, making it a perfect accompaniment to Ethiopian cuisine. Whether you have ties to Ethiopian culture or simply want to explore the intriguing flavors of this traditional flatbread, making injera from scratch can be a fascinating and rewarding culinary experience.

- The examples and recipes of dishes that use injera in Ethiopia and Eritrea

Injera is a staple food in Ethiopia and Eritrea, and it has been a significant part of their culinary traditions for centuries. Not only is it a versatile and delicious food item, but it also holds cultural and social significance.

Injera is a large, sourdough flatbread that's made from teff flour, a gluten-free grain that's native to these regions. Traditionally, it is cooked on a hot clay plate known as a mitad or a special stove called a mogogo. The process of making injera is quite intricate and time-consuming, as it usually involves fermenting the batter for a few days to develop its distinct sour taste.

One popular dish that incorporates injera is called the Tikel Gomen. Tikel Gomen is a traditional Ethiopian cabbage dish that is typically served on top of injera. To prepare this dish, cabbages and potatoes are sautéed with onions and cooked in a flavorful broth made from turmeric, ginger, and garlic. The creamy and spicy nature of the Tikel Gomen pairs perfectly with the sourness of injera and creates a hearty and satisfying meal.

Another popular dish that showcases the versatility of injera is called Doro Wat. Doro Wat is a spicy chicken stew that is often considered the national dish of Ethiopia. The stew is prepared by slow-cooking chicken in a flavorful blend of berbere spice mix, onions, garlic, ginger, and other aromatic spices. The injera is usually used as a utensil in this dish, where people tear off pieces of the flatbread and use it to scoop up the rich and spicy stew. The combination of flavors and textures in Doro Wat, along with the soft and spongy nature of injera, creates a unique eating experience.

Aside from these savory dishes, injera is also used in various desserts and snacks. Injera can be made into a sweet dish known as beles or tihlo. Beles is prepared by cutting injera into small pieces and coating them with honey or butter and then baking until crispy. Tihlo, on the other hand, is made from grinding injera into a flour-like consistency and then mixing it with honey or sugar, butter, and roasted barley flour.

Injera's unique texture and flavor make it a versatile ingredient that can be used in a variety of dishes. Its sourness adds a tangy and distinct taste to any meal. Over the years, different regions within Ethiopia and Eritrea have developed their own variations of injera-based dishes, reflecting the diversity and creativity of the cuisine in these countries.

Whether it's paired with stews, used as a vessel for scooping up flavorful sauces, or transformed into sweet treats, injera remains a fundamental part of the culinary heritage of Ethiopia and Eritrea. Its popularity has also spread beyond these countries' borders, garnering international recognition and appreciation for its extraordinary taste and cultural significance.

Chapter 7: Ogi- The origin and popularity of ogi in Nigeria and other West African countries

In Nigeria and several other West African countries, ogi occupies a prominent position in the food culture. This fermented cereal-based food, also known as pap, akamu, or eko among different ethnic groups, has a long history and is consumed by a significant percentage of the population. This chapter explores the origin and popularity of ogi, delving into its cultural significance and nutritional benefits.

Historical Background:

The origin of ogi can be traced back to ancient times when West African societies relied on locally available food sources, particularly cereals like millet, sorghum, maize, and rice. The process of fermenting these cereals to create a thick, porridge-like substance emerged as a way to increase the longevity and palatability of the grains. Ogi became an essential component of the diet, especially during times of scarcity or to augment the nutritional value of other meals.

Cultural Significance and Practices:

The popularity of ogi goes beyond mere sustenance. Traditional societies in Nigeria and West Africa hold celebrations and ceremonies that revolve around the preparation and consumption of this cherished dish. It serves as a symbol of unity, community, and gratefulness for food. For example, during childbirth, ogi is often prepared and shared among relatives and neighbors to celebrate the joyous occasion. In some ethnic groups, ogi is also used in rituals and sacrifices to appease ancestral spirits.

Preparation and Processing Techniques:

The preparation of ogi involves various processing techniques that have been passed down through generations. The grains are first soaked, sometimes for extended periods, to aid in the softening and initial fermentation. After grinding the soaked grains to form a paste, it is typically cooked and continuously stirred over low heat until it thickens to form a smooth consistency. Some communities hand-grind the cereals using traditional tools like the mortar and pestle, adding a touch of authenticity to the process.

Nutritional Value and Health Benefits:

Ogi offers multiple nutritional benefits due to both the fermentation process and the cereals used. Fermentation enriches the gruel by enhancing its nutrient content, especially vitamins of the B complex and beneficial microbes. The resulting product becomes easier to digest and improves gut health due to the presence of probiotics. Additionally, the cereals used in ogi contain high levels of dietary fiber, which aids digestion, and provide a rich source of carbohydrates and essential minerals.

Popularity and Variations:

The popularity of ogi extends well beyond Nigeria's borders, with other West African countries like Ghana, Benin, Togo, and Sierra Leone incorporating their own variations of the dish. These variations may use different cereals, such as maize or rice, resulting in diverse flavors and textures. Unlike the traditional way of consuming ogi as a standalone dish, modern variations incorporate toppings like sugar, milk, honey, or fruits, catering to evolving tastes and preferences.

———◉———

OGI, A FERMENTED CEREAL-based food with a rich history dating back centuries, holds a special place in Nigerian and West African food culture. Its origin from local cereals and its cultural significance as a symbol of unity and celebration make it an inseparable part of community practices and traditional ceremonies. Moreover, the nutritional value and health benefits derived from fermentation ensure its continued popularity and consumption. The variations and adaptations of ogi in neighboring countries contribute to the vibrant culinary landscape of West Africa, bridging connections and emphasizing shared traditions.

- The ingredients and methods of making ogi from fermented maize, millet, or sorghum

Ogi, also known as akamu or ogiri, is a traditional Nigerian fermented cereal pudding. It is made from fermented maize, millet, or sorghum, and is known for its thick and smooth consistency. Ogi is not only a popular breakfast dish, but it is also used as a weaning food for infants and a soothing meal for those with digestive issues.

To make ogi, you will need the following ingredients and equipment:

Ingredients:

1. Maize, millet, or sorghum grains
2. Water
3. Cowpea grits (optional, for added protein)
4. Ginger or garlic (optional, for flavor)
5. Sugar or honey (optional, for sweetness)

Equipment:

1. Large bowl
2. Grinding machine or blending equipment
3. Fermentation jar with lid
4. Nylon sieve or cheesecloth
5. Clean pots for cooking

Now, let's discuss the process of making ogi step-by-step:

Step 1: Clean and soak the grains

Start by cleaning the grains thoroughly in water. Remove any dirt, pebbles, or other foreign substances. Once cleaned, soak the grains in water overnight or for at least 10-12 hours. This process softens the grains and makes them easier to grind.

Step 2: Grinding the grains

After the soaking period, drain the water from the grains. Transfer them into a grinding machine or blender and process until they become a smooth paste. Ensure that there are no lumps left. If using ginger or garlic, add them to the blending process to enhance the flavor.

Step 3: Fermentation

Transfer the paste into a large bowl, and then gradually add water while stirring continuously. The mixture should have a slightly watery consistency, just like pancake batter. At this point, you can also add cowpea grits if you desire higher protein content in your ogi.

Cover the bowl with a clean cloth and let it ferment for 1-3 days. The length of the fermentation process depends on your preference. The longer it ferments, the more sour and tangy the ogi becomes. To prevent contamination during fermentation, make sure to keep the mixture in a cool, dark place and place a lid over the bowl.

Step 4: Straining the ogi

After the fermentation period ends, the mixture will separate into two layers- a watery liquid on top, and a thick sediment at the bottom. Carefully pour the watery liquid off the top using a nylon sieve or cheesecloth. This liquid, known as the 'whitewater,' can be discarded, or it can be used to cook other dishes if desired.

Next, strain the thick sediment at the bottom of the bowl through the sieve or cheesecloth. This sediment is the main ogi paste used for cooking. Squeeze out any excess liquid and discard it, or set it aside for using in thickening other meals.

Step 5: Cooking the ogi

Pour the strained ogi paste into a clean pot and place it on medium heat. Continuous stirring is necessary to prevent the mixture from forming lumps. As the ogi cooks, it gradually thickens. Adjust the heat if necessary to ensure even cooking.

When the ogi reaches your desired consistency, remove it from the heat. At this point, sugar or honey can be added to sweeten the pudding if desired.

Step 6: Serving and storing

Allow the ogi to cool down for a few minutes before serving. It can be enjoyed on its own or with other accompaniments like milk, fruits, or fried pastries.

Any leftover ogi should be stored in airtight containers in the refrigerator. It will stay fresh for 2-3 days, but make sure to reheat it before consuming.

In conclusion, making ogi from fermented maize, millet, or sorghum requires careful preparation, fermentation, and cooking. With its thick and smooth texture, it is a versatile dish enjoyed by people of all ages in Nigeria and across Africa.

- The examples and recipes of dishes that use ogi in Nigeria and other West African countries

In Nigeria and other West African countries, ogi (also known as akamu or pap) plays a significant role in the culinary culture of the region. This local fermented cereal pudding is a versatile and nutritious ingredient, making it a popular choice for both everyday meals and traditional recipes. Below, we present you with a variety of examples and recipes that demonstrate the diverse uses of ogi in West African cuisine.

1. Ogi/Pap as a Breakfast Delight:

- Ogi usually serves as a thickener for different porridge options such as cornmeal (ogi baba), millet (ogi wara), or sorghum (ogi saa). These porridges are commonly enjoyed for breakfast, providing a delicious and filling start to the day.

- To prepare ogi for breakfast, begin by soaking either corn, millet, or sorghum grains overnight. Afterward, mill the grains into a smooth flour. Mix the flour with water and strain it into a container, making sure to remove any lumps or hard particles. Boil the strained liquid and continue stirring until it thickens into a smooth and consistent porridge.

2. Ogi/Pap-based Beverages:

- In addition to being enjoyed as a porridge, ogi is used to create refreshing and nutritious beverages. For example, "Kunu" is a popular Nigerian drink made by adding blended tiger nuts, peanuts, or dates to fortified ogi. This combo is then mixed with water, sweetened to taste, and served cold. Kunu not only quenches thirst but also provides a good source of energy.

3. Fermented Ogi/Pap:

- Fermenting ogi prolongs its shelf life and enhances its flavor. This fermented version serves as a base for several Togolese dishes. A recipe called "Azedui" incorporates fermented ogi with cooked veggies, spices like ginger and garlic, and possibly fish or meat. The mixture is then cooked until it thickens into a savory stew-like consistency.

4. Ogi/Pap in Soup:

- Ogi can also be used as a thickening agent in soups and stews, adding a unique flavor and texture to the dishes. For instance, in Ghana, "Ntamie" is a popular soup made from the combination of ogi, Okra, and fish or smoked fish. This hearty and wholesome soup is commonly served with banku, a local fermented corn dumpling.

- To prepare Ntamie, blend ogi flour with water, strain it to remove lumps, and set aside. In a separate pot, cook fish or smoked fish in seasoned broth until tender, then add shredded okra. Stir in the ogi mixture and simmer until it thickens. Serve piping hot with banku.

5. Ogi/Pap Dumplings or Fritters:

- Another creative way to use ogi is by forming it into dumplings or fritters. In Nigeria, "Famore" is a delicacy made with a mixture of ogi, water, salt, onions, and sometimes peppers. The batter is then poured onto a hot greased pan in dollops, resembling small pancakes, which are cooked until golden brown on both sides. Famore can be served with honey, syrup, or enjoyed on its own.

These examples and recipes merely scratch the surface of the immense variety of Ogi/Pap-based dishes throughout West Africa. From breakfast porridges to savory stews and delectable dumplings, ogi offers plenty of opportunities for culinary creativity and exploration in this region. Whether you're a food enthusiast seeking to experience the flavors of West Africa or an individual interested in expanding your culinary repertoire, delving into the world of ogi-based dishes is sure to be a delightful and rewarding endeavor.

Chapter 8: Garri- The origin and popularity of garri in Nigeria and other West African countries

Garri, a popular staple food in Nigeria and other West African countries, holds a significant position in the region's culinary landscape. Made from cassava, garri is a versatile and nutritious food product that is widely consumed across different socioeconomic groups. This chapter aims to delve into the rich history and tradition surrounding the production, consumption, and popularity of garri within Nigeria and its neighboring countries.

1. The Origin of Garri:

1.1 Historical Roots:

The origin of garri can be traced back to Nigeria, specifically the southern part of the country, where cassava was first introduced during the Portuguese colonization in the 16th century. The capability of cassava to grow well in tropical climates and its resilience against drought and pests ensured its widespread cultivation in Nigeria and neighboring West African regions. These favorable conditions led to the development and refinement of garri production techniques and the eventual emergence of garri as a staple food.

1.2 Transition to Garri:

Originally, the consumption of fresh cassava was prevalent, but as time went by, local communities began processing it into garri to extend its shelf life. The process involves peeling the cassava root, grating the pulp, fermenting it, and then roasting it to produce the final product – garri. This processed form of cassava was found to be not only more convenient but also offered additional health benefits.

2. Making Garri: Production Process and Techniques:

2.1 Harvesting and Peeling:

The production of garri starts with the harvesting of mature cassava roots. These tubers are carefully uprooted from the ground, washed, and then peeled to remove the protective outer layers. Traditionally, this peeling process was done by hand, employing skilled laborers proficient in removing the cassava's skin without cutting too deep into the pulpy flesh.

2.2 Grating:

Once peeled, the cassava tubers are grated either manually using a grating board or processed using mechanical graters. The graters help transform the cassava into a mash-like consistency, minimizing efforts and increasing efficiency during the subsequent production stages.

2.3 Fermentation:

After grating, the mash is placed in woven bags or wrapped in banana leaves and left to ferment for a period varying from one to several days. This step contributes to the sour taste of garri and allows beneficial microorganisms present in the environment to convert the cassava's cyanogenic glycosides to safe and edible forms.

2.4 Dewatering and Roasting:

During fermentation, pressure is applied to squeeze out the liquid from the cassava mash. Traditional means such as placing weights atop the bags or utilizing wooden presses are employed for dewatering. Once dewatered, the semi-dry mash is roasted over an open fire or on hot plates until it turns golden brown or brown.

2.5 Milling and Packaging:

The roasted garri is further milled into fine particles, either manually through pounding with a mortar and pestle or using mechanical mills, to achieve uniform grain sizes. Finally, the milled garri is sieved to remove any undesirable particles and then packaged in bags or food-grade containers suitable for transportation and storage.

3. Nutritional Value and Culinary Uses of Garri:

3.1 Nutritional Composition:

Garri is not only renowned for its taste and versatility but also its nutritional value. It is predominantly a carbohydrate-rich food, providing energy to individuals across different age groups. Furthermore, the fermentation process increases the bioavailability of certain nutrients, making them more easily absorbed by the human body.

3.2 Culinary Uses:

Garri serves as a base ingredient for numerous West African dishes, of which the most popular is generally referred to as "eba" or "gari." Eba is solid garri served with a variety of soups or stews made from vegetables, meats, or fish. It can be mixed with hot water to form a pudding-like consistency, creating a popular breakfast known as "garri soakings." Additionally, garri is sometimes used as a complementary ingredient in cakes, pastries, and alcoholic beverages.

4. Popularity and Cultural Significance:

4.1 Economic Impact:

Garri production and consumption have a substantial economic impact on Nigeria and other West African countries. It serves as an important source of income for cassava farmers, processors, and traders, providing livelihoods for many individuals involved in the garri value chain.

4.2 Cultural Significance:

Garri is deeply ingrained in West African culture, making it an integral part of social gatherings, ceremonies, and festivals. It is present at traditional weddings, religious events, and family celebrations. The versatility of garri makes it accessible and adaptable across various regions and socioeconomic groups, bringing communities together through this shared culinary bond.

⟹ ⬤ ⟸

GARRI, WITH ITS FASCINATING origins and widespread popularity in Nigeria and other West African countries, holds a distinct place in the local culture and culinary traditions. Its versatility, nutritional value, and economic significance make it a staple food ingredient and a symbol of communal identity. Understanding the history and production techniques of garri provides insights into the rich cultural heritage it embodies, ensuring its continued prominence for generations to come.

- The ingredients and methods of making garri from fermented cassava

Garri is a popular West African food made from fermented cassava. The process of making garri involves several steps, starting from harvesting and peeling the cassava tubers and ending with the production of the final product, which is a dry granular flour-like substance. In this article, we will explore the different ingredients and methods used to make garri.

Ingredients:

- Cassava tubers: These are the main ingredient for making garri. Cassava is a starchy root vegetable widely cultivated in tropical regions.

- Water: The cassava tubers need to be washed and soaked in water during the process of making garri.

- Banana leaves or plastic bags: These are used to line the presser during the fermentation and drying process.

Methods:

1. Harvesting and peeling:

The first step in making garri is to harvest mature cassava tubers. The tubers are then peeled to remove the outer skin, revealing the white starchy flesh inside. The peelings are usually used for animal feed or compost.

2. Washing and soaking:

After peeling, the cassava tubers are thoroughly washed to remove any soil or dirt. They are then soaked in clean water for a period of 1-3 days. This soaking process helps to soften the cassava tubers and initiates the fermentation process.

3. Fermentation:

Once the cassava tubers are soaked, they are ready for fermentation. Traditionally, the soaked tubers are piled onto large mats covered with banana leaves. The tubers are left to ferment for 3-5 days, during which natural bacteria and yeasts convert the starches in the cassava into lactic acid. This fermentation process gives garri its distinct sour taste. In modern production processes, fermentation can be accelerated by using commercial starter cultures.

4. Pressing:

After fermentation, the cassava tubers are ready to be pressed. Traditionally, a large wooden presser called a "pounder" or "garri press" is used. The fermented tubers are placed onto the presser, covered with banana leaves or plastic bags, and pressure is applied to squeeze out the liquid from the tubers. The liquid is known as "cassava wastewater" or "cassava effluent" and can be used for various purposes like fertilizer or animal feed.

5. Drying:

Once the liquid is squeezed out, the resulting wet mash is spread out on large mats or trays to dry in the sun. In some modern production processes, mechanical dryers are used for faster drying. The cassava mash is periodically turned over to ensure even drying. This drying process can take anywhere from a few days to a week, depending on the weather conditions.

6. Milling and sieving:

Once the cassava mash is completely dry, it is ready to be milled into a fine powder. Traditional methods involve pounding the dried mash with a mortar and pestle, while modern methods use mechanical grinders or milling machines. The milled garri is then passed through a sieve to remove any large particles or fibers, resulting in a fine granular flour-like substance.

7. Packaging:

The final step in making garri is packaging. The garri is usually packed into airtight bags or containers to maintain its freshness and to prevent moisture absorption. It can then be stored for future use or sold in the market.

Garri is a versatile food that can be consumed in various ways. It can be soaked in water or eaten with hot water to form a paste-like consistency known as "eba." It can also be used as a crunchy topping for dishes or as a main ingredient in snacks like "garri cookies" or "garri cereal." It is not only a staple food in many West African countries but also gaining popularity in other parts of the world due to its unique taste and nutritional benefits.

In conclusion, garri production involves a series of steps, from harvesting and peeling the cassava tubers to fermenting, pressing, drying, milling, sieving, and packaging. The process combines traditional knowledge and modern techniques to produce a nutritious and widely consumed food product.

- The examples and recipes of dishes that use garri in Nigeria and other West African countries

Garri, a popular staple food in Nigeria and other West African countries, is made from cassava tubers. It has a light yellow color and is coarsely ground into a grainy texture. Apart from being a major source of carbohydrates, garri is rich in fiber, vitamins, and minerals, making it a nutritious and versatile ingredient.

In Nigeria, garri is commonly consumed in various forms, including "garri soakings" or "garri mixtures." These quintessential street snacks are made by mixing garri with other ingredients. Here are a few examples:

1. Garri and Sugar Soaking: This simple and delicious combination entails mixing garri with sugar and cold water. This mixture is typically enjoyed as a quick and refreshing snack on a hot day.

2. Garri and Groundnut Soaking: Another popular snacking option is made by combining garri with roasted groundnuts (peanuts). This mixture provides a delightful and crunchy texture with a fantastic blend of flavors.

3. Garri and Coconut Soaking: For those who love the tropical sweetness of coconuts, garri and coconut soaking is a delightful treat. Along with coconut flakes and garri, this dish is usually drizzled with a bit of water to soften the garri and enhance its taste.

Apart from these delicious snacking options, garri is also incorporated into various traditional West African dishes. These recipes highlight the versatility and adaptability of garri:

1. Eba: Eba is a popular Nigerian dish made with garri. It is essentially a thick, lump-free dough, similar to a stiff porridge. Garri is gradually added to boiling water while stirring continuously until a firm consistency is achieved. Eba is commonly served with soups or stews, such as egusi soup or okra soup.

2. Gari Foto: Gari Foto is a traditional Ghanaian recipe that features garri as a salad-like dish. It is prepared by tossing garri with finely chopped vegetables

like tomatoes, onions, bell peppers, and sometimes shredded fish or meat. It is dressed with a tangy vinaigrette-like sauce made with lime or lemon juice, vegetable oil, chili pepper, and salt. Gari Foto offers a refreshing and nutritious option that can be served as a standalone meal or a side dish.

3. Fufu and Akpu: Fufu and Akpu are starchy dough-like dishes made with boiled garri, plantains, or yam flour. These dough balls are served with a variety of soups and stews and are a common feature of many West African meals.

Garri's versatility and widespread use in Nigerian and West African cuisine make it a beloved ingredient. Whether enjoyed as a simple snack or incorporated into elaborate culinary creations, garri plays a significant role in the cultural and gastronomic landscape of the region.

Chapter 9: Amasi- The origin and popularity of amasi in South Africa and other Southern African countries

Chapter 9 delves into the rich history, origin, and widespread popularity of amasi, a traditional African fermented milk beverage. The chapter explores its significance in South African and other Southern African cultures, delving into the rituals, traditions, and health benefits associated with this unique and beloved dairy product.

1. The Origins of Amasi:

a. Amasi finds its roots in the African continent, with early evidence of fermented milk consumption dating back thousands of years.

b. Nomadic communities and herders in Southern Africa commonly made amasi as a preservation method to extend the shelf life of milk, enabling sustenance during times of scarcity.

c. The traditional techniques of making amasi involved leaving unpasteurized milk to ferment spontaneously at ambient temperatures, allowing the growth of beneficial bacteria.

2. The Fermentation Process and Cultural Significance:

a. The fermentation process of amasi is a vital aspect of traditional African cultures, symbolizing community values, connection to nature, and ancestral bonds.

b. Cultures across Southern Africa have their distinct symbolic and ceremonial associations with amasi, creating a sense of cultural identity and belonging.

c. The production of amasi is often a community affair where knowledge is shared and passed down through generations, reinforcing cultural heritage.

3. Amasi's Rise in Popularity:

a. Amasi has traditionally been consumed by mainly rural communities. However, over the years, it has gained popularity beyond rural areas and now transcends socio-economic boundaries.

b. The global trend towards natural and traditional foods has played a significant role in the recent surge in popularity of amasi.

c. The nutritional value of amasi, rich in probiotics, vitamins, and minerals, has led to an increased interest from health-conscious consumers.

4. Commercial Production and Industrialization:

a. With the rising demand for amasi, there has been an increase in commercial production, leading to industrialization within the dairy sector.

b. Modern production techniques involve adding specific probiotic cultures to milk, replicating the traditional fermentation process on a larger scale.

c. While commercialization has brought amasi to urban areas and international markets, some argue that it has resulted in a loss of authenticity and traditional knowledge.

5. Health Benefits of Amasi:

a. Amasi is recognized for its numerous health benefits, including improved gut health due to its high probiotic content.

b. The presence of beneficial bacteria in amasi aids digestion, strengthens immunity and helps prevent intestinal infections.

c. Consumption of amasi has also been linked to reduced lactose intolerance symptoms for those individuals who struggle with digesting milk.

CHAPTER 9 HIGHLIGHTS the origin and widespread popularity of amasi, a traditional African fermented milk beverage. From its humble origins as a preservation method, amasi has evolved into a culturally significant and commercially viable product. Its heritage, health benefits, and association with communal traditions have contributed to its current widespread consumption and growing international recognition. However, as amasi transitions into a more commercially produced commodity, it is important to preserve its authenticity and respect the traditional knowledge passed down through generations.

- The ingredients and methods of making amasi from fermented milk

Amasi is a traditional fermented milk product that is widely consumed and cherished in various parts of Africa, particularly in Southern African countries like South Africa and Zimbabwe. It is similar to yogurt but has a slightly different taste and texture. The production of amasi involves a combination of specific ingredients and a unique method of fermentation, which results in its distinct characteristics.

To make amasi, the primary ingredient is fresh cow's milk. However, in some regions, goat's milk or a mixture of cow's and goat's milk is also used. The milk used for amasi production must be clean and free from any preservatives or antibiotics. This ensures that the fermentation process is successful and produces a high-quality end product.

The fermentation of the milk is initiated by the addition of a "starter culture." Traditionally, amasi is made using an initial small amount of previously fermented milk, which serves as the starter culture for the fresh batch. This starter culture contains beneficial bacteria, including species of Lactic Acid Bacteria (LAB), such as Lactococcus and Streptococcus, which convert lactose (milk sugar) into lactic acid.

To prepare the starter culture for amasi production, a small quantity of previously fermented amasi is placed in a clean container. This acts as a seed culture to inoculate the fresh milk with beneficial bacteria. The container is covered loosely to prevent contamination while allowing air circulation.

Once the starter is prepared, it is added to the desired quantity of fresh milk. The milk mixture is then mixed thoroughly to ensure even distribution of the starter culture. The milk and the starter culture are left to ferment at room temperature, typically for a period of 24 to 48 hours. However, the fermentation time may vary depending on the temperature and desired taste. In warmer environments, fermentation can occur more rapidly.

During the fermentation process, the beneficial bacteria convert lactose into lactic acid, which gives amasi its characteristic tangy taste. The lactic acid also facilitates the coagulation of milk proteins, resulting in the thick consistency of amasi. The fermentation process also leads to the growth of other flavors and compounds that contribute to the unique taste of amasi, including diacetyl, acetaldehyde, and esters.

Once the desired level of fermentation is achieved, the fermented milk is refrigerated to halt further acid production and to preserve its taste and texture. The resulting amasi is thick, creamy, and has a sour taste, similar to yogurt but more acidic.

Amasi can be enjoyed in various ways. It can be consumed on its own as a nutritious and probiotic-rich drink, or it can be used as an ingredient in culinary preparations such as smoothies, soups, or even baked goods. Its versatility and health benefits, including boosting digestion and supporting a healthy gut microbiome, have contributed to its popularity throughout generations.

In conclusion, the process of making amasi from fermented milk involves the combination of fresh milk, a starter culture, and a specific fermentation method. The fermentation by beneficial bacteria results in a rich, tangy, and creamy product that is enjoyed by many as a delicious and nutritious dairy delight.

- The examples and recipes of dishes that use amasi in South Africa and other Southern African countries

Amasi, a traditional fermented milk product, is widely consumed and cherished in South Africa and other Southern African countries. Its popularity is not only attributed to its unique flavor and texture but also to its versatility in cooking, as it can be incorporated into a wide range of dishes. In this article, we will explore some remarkable examples and mouthwatering recipes that showcase the utilization of amasi in Southern African cuisine.

One popular dish that features amasi is the famous South African staple called Mielie Pap. It is a simple yet satisfying porridge made from maize meal and water, often served alongside grilled meats or stews. Traditionally, amasi is mixed into the pap, creating a creamy and tangy texture that complements the rich flavors of the accompanying dishes. The addition of amasi not only imparts a pleasant taste but also enhances the nutritional value of the meal, as it is a good source of calcium, protein, and probiotics.

Another beloved dish in Southern Africa that incorporates amasi is Chakalaka. It is a fiery and flavorful relish composed of various vegetables such as onions, tomatoes, peppers, and beans. The amasi not only acts as a base for the relish but also helps to balance out the spiciness and add a creamy element to the dish. The combination of the tangy amasi and the vibrant flavors of the Chakalaka make for a tantalizing experience that is best enjoyed with braai (barbecue) meats or as a condiment alongside a range of dishes.

Moving on to desserts, amasi is frequently used in baking as well. For instance, a classic recipe is Amasi scones. These delightful treats are made by combining flour, sugar, baking powder, salt, and butter, then adding a generous amount of amasi to bind the dry ingredients together. The result is a batch of light and fluffy scones with a slight tanginess and an undertone of sweetness. They are often served with a dollop of jam or cream and enjoyed for breakfast or as an afternoon snack.

For those with a sweet tooth, Amarula Panna Cotta with Amasi is an irresistible choice. This luxurious dessert encompasses the richness of Amarula, a popular cream liqueur made from the fruit of the Marula tree, and the smoothness of amasi. The Amarula Panna Cotta is set using gelatin, cream, sugar, and Amarula liqueur, and then garnished with a spoonful of amasi before serving. The combination of flavors here is outstanding – the creamy and boozy Amarula pairs excellently with the tangy and velvety amasi, creating a truly indulgent treat that will leave you craving for more.

These are just a few examples of the countless dishes and recipes that utilize amasi in South Africa and other Southern African countries. Whether it's breakfast, lunch, dinner, or even dessert, amasi adds a distinct flavor and texture that enhances the culinary experiences of millions of people in the region. So, next time you have a chance to try an amasi-based dish, seize the opportunity and savor the delightful taste and cultural significance that it brings to Southern African cuisine!

Chapter 10: Biltong- The origin and popularity of biltong in South Africa and other Southern African countries

Biltong is a popular type of cured meat commonly enjoyed in many Southern African countries, with its origins deeply rooted in South African history and tradition. In this chapter, we will explore the fascinating history, production process, and cultural significance of biltong, as well as its enduring popularity among locals and its growing recognition worldwide.

1. Historical Origins of Biltong:

The origins of biltong can be traced back to the early days of European migrations to Southern Africa. Dutch settlers, known as Voortrekkers, made their way to the region in the mid-17th century, bringing with them their meat preservation techniques. These techniques were adapted to suit the local climate and available resources, resulting in the creation of biltong.

2. Production Process of Biltong:

Traditionally, biltong was made using game meat, such as venison or wild game. However, today a variety of meats, including beef, ostrich, and even fish, can be used to make this flavorful snack. The meat is typically marinated in a mixture of vinegar, salt, coriander, and other spices before being air-dried for several days. This slow curing process allows the meat to develop its distinctive rich flavor and tender texture.

3. Cultural Significance of Biltong:

Biltong is deeply ingrained in South African culture and is often associated with outdoor activities such as hunting, hiking, and braai (barbecue). It is commonly used as a snack during social gatherings, sports events, and even as a staple in traditional cuisine. Biltong is seen as a symbol of community and heritage, connecting South Africans to their historical roots and culinary traditions.

4. Popularity of Biltong in Southern African Countries:

While biltong is most commonly associated with South Africa, its popularity extends beyond the borders of the country. In neighboring countries like Namibia and Zimbabwe, biltong holds similar cultural significance and remains a popular snack and protein source. Its versatility, long shelf life, and rich flavor profile have made it a perfect fit for the diverse culinary preferences of the Southern African region.

5. Global Recognition of Biltong:

In recent years, biltong has gained international recognition, capturing the interest of food enthusiasts and health-conscious consumers worldwide. Its natural production process, resulting in a preservative-free and protein-packed snack, has made it an attractive alternative to heavily processed meat products. With the rise of food tourism and the growing popularity of ethnic cuisines, biltong has found its place in gourmet markets, artisanal food fairs, and even in high-end restaurants abroad.

⎯⎯◉⎯⎯

BILTONG, A CURED MEAT snack with its origins deeply rooted in Dutch and South African history, has become a beloved food in Southern African countries. Its distinct flavor, cultural significance, and long-standing tradition has captured the hearts and taste buds of locals and foreigners alike. As it continues to gain global recognition, biltong remains a testament to the rich culinary heritage of Southern Africa, connecting people through its shared enjoyment and appreciation.

- The ingredients and methods of making biltong from fermented meat

Biltong – a South African staple food made from fermented meat – is gaining popularity worldwide due to its unique taste, extended shelf life, and high nutritional value. This traditional cured meat snack originally evolved as a preservation method in the hot, dry climate of Southern Africa. In this article, we will explore the ingredients and methods involved in making biltong from fermented meat.

Ingredients:

1. Quality Meat: Biltong can be made from various types of meat, but beef is the most commonly used choice. The cut of meat should have a good balance of fat and lean. Popular choices include silverside, topside, or even rump steak. In some cases, game meats like venison or ostrich are also used.

2. Spices: Key spices used in biltong marinades include coriander, black pepper, salt, brown sugar, and vinegar. These spices add depth of flavor and help in the curing process.

3. Vinegar: Vinegar acts as both a flavor enhancer and an antimicrobial agent. The acidity helps inhibit the growth of harmful bacteria during the curing process.

Methods:

1. Preparation: Start by selecting a good quality piece of meat and trim off any excess fat. Slice the meat into long, thin strips across the grain for a tender finished product. The thickness of the strips can be personal preference, but roughly ½ inch is a common thickness.

2. Marinating: Prepare a marinade using a combination of spices, salt, brown sugar, and vinegar. Some variations might include additional flavorings like Worcestershire sauce or chili. Generously coat the meat strips with the marinade, making sure each piece is fully covered. Place the marinated meat in a sealable container, making sure to drain excess liquid. For maximum flavor absorption, marinate refrigerated for at least 4 hours, or overnight if possible.

3. Drying: After marinating, remove the meat from the container and pat it dry with a paper towel to remove any dripping marinade. You can brush off any excess spices if desired. Using a biltong drying box or an alternative drying environment, hang the strips with sufficient air circulation. The meat should be suspended so the pieces don't touch each other. Optimal conditions for drying biltong include a cool, dry, and well-ventilated area that is not exposed to direct sunlight.

4. Fermentation: During the drying process, natural air fermentation occurs. The long drying time allows good bacteria to work on the meat, breaking down proteins and creating a unique flavor profile. This fermentation stage can be anywhere from two days to two weeks, depending on the desired texture and taste. The meat should be periodically checked to ensure it is drying consistently and does not have any signs of spoilage.

5. Done-ness: Once the biltong strips have dried to your liking, check the consistency by pressing them between your fingers. The ideal biltong should be firm, but still slightly pliable. If it is too dry or too moist, adjust your drying time for the next batch.

6. Storage: Once the biltong is ready, store it in an airtight container or vacuum-sealed bags. Properly stored biltong can last for months, making it a convenient snack option.

Biltong is not only a delicious and satisfying meat treat, but it also provides a substantial amount of protein, making it a popular choice for athletes and health-conscious individuals. So next time you're craving a unique savory snack, give biltong a try, and impress your taste buds with this delicious cured meat delicacy.

- The examples and recipes of dishes that use biltong in South Africa and other Southern African countries

Biltong is a traditional and popular meat snack enjoyed across Southern Africa, particularly in South Africa, Zimbabwe, Botswana, and Namibia. This delectable cured and dried meat is widely savored as a quick, high-protein snack or an ingredient that adds a unique and flavorful twist to various dishes. With its long history rooted in the region, biltong has become an integral part of Southern African cuisine. In this article, we will explore the examples and recipes of dishes that utilize biltong in South Africa and the surrounding countries.

1. Biltong Slices:

The simplest and most classic way to enjoy biltong is to savor it as a snack on its own. Purchase a bag of biltong slices or cut your own from a biltong slab. The thin slices offer a satisfying and flavorsome experience, showcasing the rich taste of the prime beef or game used in its preparation.

2. Biltong Salad:

Biltong can be the star ingredient in a hearty and nutritious salad. Combine fresh salad greens or spinach leaves with sliced tomatoes, onions, avocado, and cucumber. Top the salad with generous amounts of biltong slices and drizzle with a tangy dressing of your choice, such as balsamic vinaigrette. The biltong's robust flavor complements the freshness of the vegetables, creating a delectable fusion.

3. Biltong Pasta:

Biltong can lend its uniqueness to a range of pasta dishes. Cook your favorite pasta al dente and set it aside. In a pan, sauté finely chopped onions, garlic, and bell peppers. Add sliced mushrooms and cook until lightly browned. Toss in biltong strips and stir-fry for a few minutes. Finally, combine the cooked pasta with the biltong and vegetable mixture, tossing everything together.

Season with salt, pepper, and Italian herbs for a delightful twist on an Italian favorite.

4. Biltong Potjie:

Potjiekos, a traditional South African stew, is often prepared using various meats and vegetables. For a unique twist, biltong can be incorporated into the potjie for enhanced flavor. Start by browning chunks of beef or game in a pot over open flames or on the stovetop. Once browned, add sliced onions, carrots, potatoes, and other vegetables of your choice. Add a mixture of beef or game stock and red wine, ensuring the ingredients are immersed in liquid. Then, add a handful of biltong pieces to the pot, distributing them evenly. Allow the ingredients to simmer slowly for a couple of hours until the meat is tender and the flavors meld together. Serve with freshly baked bread or rice.

5. Biltong and Cheese Platter:

Create an appetizer platter using biltong alongside an array of cheeses. Select a variety of cheeses, ranging from firm favorites like cheddar and gouda to creamy camembert and blue cheese. Arrange thin slices of biltong on a wooden board or platter, alternating with the cheeses. Serve with delicious accompaniments like crackers, breadsticks, fresh fruits, and a selection of chutneys or jams. The combinations of flavors will tantalize your taste buds and make for an indulgent and satisfying snack.

Whether enjoyed in its traditional form or creatively incorporated into various dishes, biltong brings a distinct South African touch to meals and snacks. Its unique curing and drying process make it an enduring favorite across the Southern African region. So, whether you're exploring Southern African cuisine or simply looking for a flavorful and protein-packed snack, biltong is sure to satisfy your cravings and introduce you to the taste of authentic Southern Africa.

Chapter 11: Mabisi- The origin and popularity of mabisi in Zambia and other Central African countries

Central Africa is a region known for its rich cultural heritage and diverse traditions. Amongst the many intriguing practices in this part of the world, the consumption of mabisi holds a special place. Mabisi, a traditional fermented milk beverage, has a profound history and has become an inseparable part of the culinary fabric of Zambia and other countries in Central Africa. In this chapter, we will delve into the origin of mabisi and explore the reasons behind its popularity in the region.

1. Historical Origins:

To understand the origin of mabisi, we must cast our gaze back into the precolonial era. The Bemba people of present-day Zambia were among the early creators and consumers of this delightful dairy beverage. Historical records reveal that mabisi was a staple in Bemba culture, fulfilling an array of purposes from nourishment during long journeys to ceremonial offerings during important social events. The intricate process of fermenting milk was initially guided by oral traditions, with knowledge passing down through generations. As the population migrated and interacted with other ethnic groups, mabisi spread to various regions of Central Africa, becoming a cherished part of different communities.

2. Traditional Production Process:

The production process of mabisi is an intricate and fascinating one. From milking cows to the final fermentation, every step contributes to its unique taste and texture. Once fresh milk is obtained, it is heated, and microbial cultures, known as starter cultures, are added. These cultures consist of a combination of lactic acid bacteria, yeasts, and molds that naturally occur in the environment. The mixture is then kept in a controlled environment, usually wrapped in banana leaves, to ferment for a period ranging from one to three days. The final product is characterized by its thick consistency, tangy flavor, and subtle effervescence.

3. Nutritional Benefits:

Apart from its cultural significance, mabisi offers a range of nutritional benefits. Fermentation transforms milk into a probiotic delight, enriching it with beneficial bacteria that aid digestion and support the immune system. Mabisi is also a good source of essential nutrients such as proteins, vitamins, and minerals. In regions where access to dairy products is limited, mabisi plays a crucial role in fulfilling nutritional requirements, especially for children and the elderly.

4. Social and Cultural Significance:

The popularity of mabisi extends beyond its nutritional properties. In Central African societies, mabisi plays a significant role in socio-cultural events and everyday life. It is common to serve mabisi during traditional ceremonies, weddings, and even as a gesture of hospitality when welcoming guests. The distinct flavor and texture of mabisi evoke a sense of familiarity, connecting individuals with their ancestral roots and preserving cultural identity. The act of sharing mabisi strengthens social bonds and fosters a sense of community amongst people.

5. Economic Significance:

Mabisi production has evolved from a merely traditional practice to an important economic activity in many Central African countries. Small-scale farmers, particularly women, are key contributors to mabisi production, nurturing their own cow herds and selling surplus milk or mabisi in local markets. The revenue generated sustains livelihoods and empowers these rural communities, serving as a means of poverty alleviation and economic upliftment.

6. Health and Hygiene Considerations:

While mabisi offers numerous benefits, health and hygiene considerations should not be discounted. Uncontrolled fermentation processes or unhygienic handling may lead to the proliferation of harmful bacteria, presenting health risks. Efforts have been made to promote regulated production practices and raise awareness about proper fermentation techniques, ensuring the quality and safety of mabisi for consumers.

MABISI, WITH ITS DEEP-rooted history and wide-ranging significance, embodies the essence of Central African culture. From its origin among the Bemba people in Zambia to its prominence in various Central African countries, mabisi has stood the test of time as a revered traditional beverage. Its nutritional benefits, social and cultural significance, economic contributions, and ongoing efforts to ensure health and hygiene make mabisi not just a symbol of Central Africa, but also a shining example of how traditional practices continue to positively impact societies in the modern world.

- The ingredients and methods of making mabisi from fermented milk

T he Art of Making Mabisi: Unveiling the Hidden Secrets of Fermented Milk

MABISI, A TRADITIONAL fermented milk drink, has been a popular beverage in various African countries for centuries. This writing aims to delve into the ingredients and methods involved in crafting this delectable and healthy dairy product. With its rich cultural significance and impressive health benefits, understanding the art of making mabisi is like unlocking a treasure trove of flavor and tradition.

I. Ingredients:

To create mabisi, the first and most important ingredient is fresh, high-quality milk. This milk can come from various sources, including cows, goats, or even camels, depending on the region and culture. The key is to source milk that is free from any additives, preservatives, or potential contaminants.

1. Starter cultures:

The magic happens when starter cultures are introduced into the milk, kickstarting the fermentation process. Starter cultures typically consist of lactic acid bacteria like Lactococcus, Lactobacillus, and Leuconostoc. These bacteria convert the lactose in milk into lactic acid, which gives mabisi its characteristic tang and aroma.

2. Previous batch of Mabisi (optional):

Traditional methods entail using the previously made batch of mabisi, known as a "mother culture," as a starter culture. This method ensures the preservation of specific desirable strains of bacteria for a consistent and authentic taste.

3. Additional ingredients (optional):

Certain cultures add ingredients like sugar, salt, or herbs to enhance the flavor profile of mabisi. However, these additions mainly cater to regional preferences and tastes.

II. Methods:

The successful creation of mabisi involves a series of steps that dictate the fermentation process. The following methods offer insights into the traditional approach, though slight variations may exist across different communities.

1. Milk collection and treatment:

Freshly milked milk is collected in a clean container and immediately processed. Any sediment or impurities are settled at the bottom before proceeding with fermentation.

2. Heated or raw milk:

Depending on the cultural variations, the collected milk can be heated or used raw. Raw milk fermentation preserves a broader range of beneficial bacteria that aid digestion, while heating the milk ensures a longer shelf life and destroys any potentially harmful microorganisms present.

3. Inoculation:

Once the milk is prepared, a starter culture is introduced. If using a previous batch of mabisi as the starter culture, a small quantity is added, while commercially-bought starter cultures come with specific instructions and measurements.

4. Incubation:

The inoculated milk is then covered loosely with a cloth or lid and left to ferment at room temperature or a slightly warm environment. The duration of fermentation can vary, typically ranging from 8 to 24 hours, allowing the proliferation of lactic acid bacteria and the conversion of lactose into lactic acid.

5. Desired consistency:

Mabisi can either have a thick or thin consistency, depending on personal preference. After the desired fermentation period, the mixture is stirred or strained to achieve the desired texture.

6. Storage:

Refrigeration halts the fermentation process and helps to preserve the drink. However, traditionally, mabisi was stored in clay pots or gourds, as they provided a conducive environment for the maturation and prolonged preservation of the drink.

MAKING MABISI IS AN art that marries tradition, nourishment, and cultural heritage. The careful selection of ingredients, precise methods, and the intrinsic link between the fermentation process and beneficial bacteria contribute to the unmatched taste and health benefits of this fascinating fermented milk drink. By recognizing and appreciating the hidden secrets of mabisi, we can foster a deeper connection to the diverse communities that have cherished this beverage for generations. So, why not embark on a mabisi-making adventure and savor the delights of this remarkable elixir?

- The examples and recipes of dishes that use mabisi in Zambia and other Central African countries

Mabisi is a traditional dairy product widely consumed in Zambia and other Central African countries. It is made from fermented milk, which not only enhances its flavor and texture but also increases its nutritional value. In this article, we will explore some examples and recipes of dishes that make use of mabisi.

1. Chibwantu: Chibwantu is a popular dish in Zambia, especially among the Bemba people. It is made by adding mabisi to cooked minced beef or chicken. The meat is usually seasoned with salt, black pepper, and, optionally, onions and tomatoes. Chibwantu is traditionally served with nshima (a thick maize porridge) or mealie meal (maize flour).

2. Mabisi Sauce: Mabisi sauce is a versatile dish that can be served with bread, rice, or potatoes. To prepare this sauce, heat some oil in a pan and sauté chopped onions and garlic until golden brown. Add diced tomatoes, green peppers, and any other vegetables you like. The secret ingredient is pouring in mabisi, which enriches the flavors and creates a creamy texture. Allow the sauce to simmer for a few minutes, add salt and other seasonings to taste, and serve hot.

3. Mabisi Salad Dressing: Mabisi can also be transformed into a tangy salad dressing. In a blender, combine mabisi with olive oil, lemon juice, freshly chopped herbs, such as parsley or basil, garlic, and salt. Blend until smooth and pour over your favorite greens, cucumbers, tomatoes, and other salad ingredients. This creamy dressing adds a unique twist to conventional salads while providing a healthy dose of probiotics.

4. Mabisi Smoothie: For a refreshing and nutritious beverage, mix together mabisi, your choice of fruits (such as mango, pineapple, and banana), and a sweetener of your choice (honey or sugar). Blend until smooth, add ice cubes if

desired, and serve chilled. This smoothie not only satisfies your taste buds but also helps you gain the benefits of mabisi and fruits.

5. Mabisi Pancakes: Surprise your taste buds by incorporating mabisi into your pancakes. Prepare your favorite pancake mix and substitute some of the milk with mabisi. The fermentation process gives the pancakes a unique and slightly tangy flavor, while also making them fluffy and moist. Serve these pancakes with butter, syrup, or fresh fruit for a delightful breakfast or brunch option.

Mabisi provides an excellent source of probiotics, vitamins, minerals, and protein. It is not only nutritious but also delicious, making it a vital part of the Central African cuisine. Whether incorporated into main dishes, sauces, or desserts, mabisi adds a distinct flavor that enhances the overall culinary experience. So, give these mabisi-based recipes a try and indulge in the rich flavors of Central Africa.

Chapter 12: Munkoyo- The origin and popularity of munkoyo in Zambia and other Central African countries

Munkoyo is a traditional African beverage that has a long history and deep cultural significance in Zambia and other Central African countries. This chapter explores the origins of munkoyo, its traditional preparation methods, and its popularity among the locals. Furthermore, it highlights the role of munkoyo in African society and its significance as a social and communal drink.

1. The Origins of Munkoyo:

1.1 Historical Background:

Munkoyo traces its origins to ancient traditional practices that have been passed down through generations in Central Africa. The beverage holds roots in various African tribes such as the Lozi, Chewa, and Lunda, with each community having slight variations in its recipe and preparation methods.

1.2 Traditional Beliefs and Rituals:

In many African cultures, munkoyo holds immense cultural and spiritual significance and is often associated with specific rituals and ancestral worship practices. It is regarded as a sacred drink meant to bring good fortune, prosperity, and blessings from the ancestors. This aspect highlights the close relationship between munkoyo and the community's spiritual beliefs.

2. Munkoyo: Preparation and Ingredients:

2.1 Ingredients:

The main ingredient used in munkoyo preparation is cassava, a root vegetable widely grown throughout Central Africa. Other ingredients such as millet, maize, or sorghum may also be added depending on regional preferences and availability. The traditional preparation methods of munkoyo emphasize the use of locally sourced, natural ingredients.

2.2 Preparation Process:

The preparation of munkoyo is a meticulous process that requires expertise and patience. Cassava roots are first peeled, washed, and grated into a fine pulp. The pulp is then fermented for several days to convert the starches into sugars, crucial for the natural fermentation process. After the fermentation period, the pulp is washed to remove any residual toxins, and the resulting liquid is sweetened and infused with various flavors, including spices and fruits.

3. Popularity of Munkoyo in Central Africa:

3.1 Cultural Significance:

Munkoyo's popularity in Central Africa goes beyond its taste and flavor. The beverage is deeply intertwined with various social and cultural practices. It is often served during essential life events such as marriages, births, and coming-of-age ceremonies, bringing communities together and fostering a sense of unity and togetherness. Munkoyo holds a sense of shared identity and heritage, strengthening the cultural fabric of Central African societies.

3.2 Health Benefits:

Munkoyo is known for its numerous health benefits. Cassava, with its high carbohydrate and mineral content, provides energy and vital nutrients. The drink is also rich in probiotics, obtained through the fermentation process, which aids in digestion and promotes gut health. Furthermore, munkoyo has become an essential component in the fight against malnutrition, particularly in rural areas where food insecurity is prevalent.

4. Contemporary Relevance of Munkoyo:

4.1 Commercial Production and Modernization:

While munkoyo has deep traditional roots, its popularity has transcended cultural boundaries. In recent years, there has been a growing interest in commercial production and commercialization of munkoyo. This has resulted in the development of modernized production techniques and greater accessibility to the drink, both domestically and internationally.

4.2 Role in Tourism and Promoting Cultural Heritage:

Munkoyo plays a significant role in promoting African cultural heritage and tourism. Many communities organize cultural festivals where munkoyo is prominently featured, giving tourists a chance to experience and learn about traditional practices. Additionally, the increasing availability of munkoyo in restaurants and markets enriches visitors' experiences while supporting local entrepreneurs and traders.

MUNKOYO'S ORIGIN AND its popularity in Zambia and Central African countries illustrate the strong cultural foundations and rich heritage of these regions. Its significance as a communal and spiritually linked beverage showcases the importance of preserving traditional practices in modern society. As munkoyo gains recognition both domestically and internationally, it offers an excellent opportunity to celebrate African culture while providing economic benefits for local communities.

- The ingredients and methods of making munkoyo from fermented millet or sorghum

Munkoyo is a traditional African drink categorized as a non-alcoholic, fermented beverage. It is popularly consumed in Zambia, Angola, and other African countries. The preparation of munkoyo involves fermenting millet or sorghum to produce a delicious and thirst-quenching beverage. In this article, we will delve into the ingredients and methods of making munkoyo, highlighting its unique and interesting aspects.

Ingredients:

1. Millet or Sorghum: Munkoyo is traditionally made using either millet or sorghum grains. These grains are abundant in African countries and serve as the base ingredient. Millet is a nutrient-dense grain that provides essential vitamins and minerals. Sorghum, on the other hand, is gluten-free, making munkoyo suitable for individuals with gluten sensitivities.

2. Water: For the fermentation process, clean water is crucial. It plays a vital role in hydrating the grains and facilitating the fermentation of millet or sorghum into a flavorful drink.

3. Activator: A munkoyo starter, locally known as kumanda or springtails, is used to initiate the fermentation process. These tiny organisms contain yeast and bacteria, which are responsible for transforming the starches in millet or sorghum into alcohol and lactic acid.

Methods:

1. Soaking and cleaning: Begin by thoroughly washing the millet or sorghum grains to remove any impurities such as dirt or stones. Once clean, place the grains in a large bowl or container.

2. Water addition: Pour clean water over the grains, fully submerging them. Use enough water to ensure that the grains are well-soaked, but not excessively watery. The grains should puff up as they absorb the water.

3. Fermentation: Add the munkoyo starter (kumanda) to the soaked grains. The dosage of starter may vary, but a typical rule of thumb is to scatter around

50-100 grams of kumanda for every kilogram of grains. This addition of the starter introduces the necessary yeast and bacteria cultures to initiate fermentation.

4. Mixing and covering: Stir the grain and water mixture thoroughly, ensuring that the starter is evenly distributed. Cover the bowl or container with a clean cloth or lid to allow airflow and prevent contamination from external sources.

5. Fermentation period: The fermentation process typically takes around 12 to 24 hours, although this duration may vary depending on the climate and ambient temperature. During this time, the yeasts and bacteria begin breaking down the starches into alcohol and lactic acid, resulting in the conversion of the mixture into a tangy, lightly effervescent drink.

6. Straining: Once the fermentation period is complete, strain the mixture through a fine sieve or cheesecloth to separate the liquid from the grains. The resulting munkoyo will have a light yellow color and a delicate, refreshing flavor profile.

7. Storage: Transfer the strained munkoyo into tight-sealing bottles or jars, and refrigerate to enhance the drink's shelf life. Proper storage ensures that the flavors continue to develop, and the acidic fermentation stays in check.

Serve chilled, and feel free to experiment with adding additional ingredients such as sugar, lemon or lime juice, ginger, or even fruit extracts to give munkoyo your own unique twist.

The process of making munkoyo from fermented millet or sorghum is not only an ancient tradition but also a testament to African culinary heritage. The resulting drink is a fantastic alternative to commercially produced beverages, as it is rich in probiotics and natural flavors. So, why not venture into the world of homemade munkoyo and explore the delights of this authentic African fermentation process?

- The examples and recipes of dishes that use munkoyo in Zambia and other Central African countries

Munkoyo, also known as maize beer or chibwantu, is a traditional fermented beverage consumed in Zambia and other Central African countries. This delightful drink has a rich history and is deeply ingrained in the culinary traditions of these regions. Not only is munkoyo a large part of the cultural heritage, but it also holds significant importance in social gatherings and ceremonies.

To prepare munkoyo, the main ingredient used is maize (corn). A porridge-like mixture is made by boiling maize meal in water until it thickens. This mixture is then transferred to a large container called a chibwantu, where it is left to ferment for a period ranging from two to four days. During fermentation, the natural yeast present in the environment converts the starches in the maize into alcohol, giving munkoyo its characteristic tangy flavor.

This homemade brew not only provides a refreshing thirst quencher but also offers several health benefits. Due to the natural fermentation process, munkoyo contains probiotics that promote gut health. It is also rich in vitamins, minerals, and antioxidants derived from maize, making it a nutritious option for locals.

While munkoyo can certainly be enjoyed on its own, it is also commonly used in the preparation of various culinary dishes. Here are a few examples:

1. Munkoyo Akabwali: This is a popular dish in Zambia made with munkoyo and pounded groundnuts. The dish is prepared by boiling munkoyo until it thickens further, after which pounded groundnuts are added to create a creamy and savory sauce. This dish is often served with fish, chicken, or meat and is enjoyed with a side of maize meal or nshima.

2. Munkoyo-Marinated Meat: Munkoyo makes for an excellent marinade for meats, especially goat and beef. The tangy flavor of the fermented beverage

helps tenderize the meat and gives it a distinct taste. After marinating the meat in the munkoyo, it can be grilled, roasted, or fried to perfection.

3. Munkoyo Bread: Munkoyo is not only limited to savory dishes; it can also be used in baking. Munkoyo bread is a unique and delicious treat where fermented munkoyo is added to the dough mixture. The resulting bread has a tangy taste and a soft texture, making it a delightful alternative to regular bread.

4. Munkoyo Salad Dressing: The tangy and slightly acidic nature of munkoyo makes it a fantastic base for salad dressings. It can be mixed with various herbs, spices, and olive oil to create a refreshing and flavorful dressing for both leafy green salads and fruit salads.

5. Munkoyo Smoothie: Munkoyo can also be used to add a tangy twist to smoothies. Blending fruits, yogurt, and a bit of munkoyo together creates a unique and refreshing beverage with a zesty kick.

These are just a few examples of the diversity of dishes that can be prepared using munkoyo in Zambia and Central African countries. With its distinctive flavor and multiple health benefits, munkoyo continues to be cherished and celebrated as a vital part of the region's culinary heritage.

Chapter 13: Mahewu- The origin and popularity of mahewu in Zimbabwe and other Southern African countries

In this chapter, we delve into the origins and increasing popularity of a traditional Southern African beverage known as mahewu. We will explore its fascinating history, cultural significance, and the various forms it takes in different countries across the region. Mahewu, a nutrient-rich fermented cereal drink, has long been a staple in the diets of many Southern African communities. Its popularity has transcended generations and borders, making it a cherished and iconic drink in this part of the world.

Historical Origins:

Mahewu, also known as amahewu or maheu, finds its roots in the ancestral kitchens and brewing traditions of the Southern African people. The exact origins of mahewu remain unknown, but it is believed to have been consumed by indigenous tribes as early as the 16th century. The traditional recipe consists of sorghum or millet, mixed with water and fermented over a period of several days. This simple yet effective method was passed down through generations, resulting in the flavorsome, slightly tangy mahewu we know today.

Cultural Significance:

Mahewu holds great cultural significance for many Southern African communities. It is often enjoyed during significant celebrations such as weddings, funerals, and other communal gatherings. The drink plays a crucial role in strengthening social bonds and creating a sense of togetherness. The act of sharing a clay pot of mahewu symbolizes unity, respect, and a connection to one's cultural heritage. In many households, mahewu is also considered a symbol of hospitality, as guests are often offered a refreshing glass upon entering a home.

Flavor and Variety:

Over time, mahewu has undergone various adaptations and is now made with different cereal grains, including maize, rice, and even wheat. This has led to a wide range of flavorful mahewu varieties available today. In Zimbabwe, for instance, plain mahewu remains the most popular version, characterized by its milky-white appearance and slightly sour taste. However, fruit-flavored variations, such as strawberry, mango, and pineapple, have gained considerable popularity, especially among the younger generation.

Mahewu's Nutritional Value:

Beyond its cultural significance and refreshing flavor, mahewu boasts commendable nutritional properties. The fermentation process involved in preparing mahewu increases its nutritional value by enhancing the availability of vitamins and other nutrients. It is an excellent source of vitamins B complex and C, as well as essential minerals like iron, calcium, and potassium.

Commercialization and Modernization:

With its growing popularity, mahewu has transitioned from a humble homemade brew to a widely commercialized beverage. Small-scale producers have emerged, creating packaged mahewu available in supermarkets, street markets, and restaurants. The commercial versions have extended the drink's shelf life while maintaining its traditional flavors. Additionally, technological advancements have allowed for mass production and distribution, minimizing the barriers of accessibility faced in the past.

Export Potential:

As the popularity of mahewu continues to expand beyond regional borders, there has been an increase in the export of this traditional beverage. The unique flavors and nutritious properties of mahewu make it an attractive option for health-conscious consumers seeking alternative beverages. Market demand for organic, fermented drinks has presented opportunities for Southern African countries to capitalize on the export potential of mahewu, contributing to their economic growth.

<hr>

THIS CHAPTER HAS PROVIDED a comprehensive overview of mahewu, ranging from its historical origins and cultural significance to its modern commercialization and export potential. As a much-loved, nutrient-rich drink, mahewu has firmly established itself as a cherished aspect of Southern African culture. Its time-honored traditions and unique flavors continue to inspire both local communities and the wider world, captivating taste buds and fostering cultures of togetherness. Mahewu proves that not only can a simple beverage quench one's thirst, but it can also carry the weight of an entire region's cultural identity.

- The ingredients and methods of making mahewu from fermented maize or sorghum

Mahewu is a traditional African beverage that is popular in many countries across the continent. It is made from fermented maize or sorghum, and it is loved for its refreshing taste and nutritional benefits. In this article, we will explore the ingredients and methods of making mahewu in detail.

Ingredients:

To make mahewu, you will need the following ingredients:

1. Maize or sorghum: The main ingredient of mahewu is either maize or sorghum. These grains are soaked in water and allowed to ferment, creating a healthy and delicious drink.

2. Sugar: Mahewu is lightly sweetened with sugar. The amount of sugar used can be adjusted according to personal preference.

3. Water: Water is an essential part of the mahewu-making process. It is used to soak the maize or sorghum and dilute the fermented mixture to achieve the desired consistency.

4. Traditional fermentation starter: To kickstart the fermentation process, a traditional starter is used. This can be easily obtained from the local market or by saving a portion of the previous batch of mahewu to act as a starter for the next batch. This starter is known as "thin pHALA."

Methods:

Here are the step-by-step instructions for making mahewu from fermented maize or sorghum:

1. Soaking: Begin by soaking the maize or sorghum in water for a few hours or overnight. This softens the grains, making it easier to blend and extract the liquid.

2. Grinding: Drain the soaked maize or sorghum and grind it using a blender or a traditional grinding stone until a smooth, fine mixture is obtained.

Add some water during the grinding process to achieve a semi-liquid consistency.

3. Straining: Strain the ground mixture through a fine mesh or muslin cloth, separating the liquid from the solid particles. It is important to extract as much liquid as possible.

4. Fermentation: Transfer the liquid into a clean, wide-mouthed container. Add sugar and the traditional fermentation starter known as "thin pHALA" to the mixture. Stir well, ensuring that all the ingredients are well incorporated. Cover the container with a clean cloth or plastic wrap, securing it tightly to keep insects and dust out.

5. Fermentation period: Allow the mixture to ferment for about 24 to 48 hours at room temperature. The fermentation time may vary depending on the desired taste and climate conditions. During this period, natural fermentation will occur, producing bubbles and a distinct tangy smell.

6. Storage: Once the fermentation period is complete, stir the fermented mixture to enhance the flavor and strain it once more to remove any remaining solids or sediments. Transfer the liquid into clean, airtight bottles or containers for storage in the refrigerator.

7. Serving: Mahewu is best served chilled. It can be enjoyed as a standalone beverage or paired with traditional African dishes like pap or isitshwala.

In conclusion, mahewu is a delightful fermented beverage made from maize or sorghum. Its ingredients are simple, natural, and easily accessible. With a bit of time and patience, anyone can enjoy the process of making this popular African drink and savor its unique flavors and nutritional benefits.

- The examples and recipes of dishes that use mahewu in Zimbabwe and other Southern African countries

The use of mahewu as a key ingredient in various traditional dishes is a common culinary practice in Zimbabwe and other Southern African countries. Mahewu is a thick, fermented porridge-like beverage made from maize meal or sorghum flour. While it is commonly consumed as a refreshing and nutritious drink on its own, it is also used in the preparation of a wide array of delicious dishes that are popular in the region. Here are a few examples of such dishes and their respective recipes:

1. Fantan: Fantan is a traditional Zimbabwean dish that features a filling made from mahewu. Typically prepared during special occasions and festive gatherings, this dish is known for its rich flavors and unique texture. Here's how to make it:

Ingredients:

- 2 cups of mahewu

- 1 cup of cooked ground beef or chicken

- 1 onion, finely chopped

- 2 tablespoons of cooking oil

- 2 cloves of garlic, minced

- 1 teaspoon of ground paprika

- Salt and pepper to taste

- Fresh cilantro or parsley for garnish

Instructions:

1. Heat the cooking oil in a frying pan over medium heat and sauté the onion and garlic until fragrant.

2. Add the cooked ground beef or chicken to the pan and cook until browned.

3. Sprinkle the paprika, salt, and pepper over the meat and stir well.

4. Pour in the mahewu and let the mixture simmer for about 10 minutes, allowing the flavors to meld together.

5. Serve the fantan hot, garnished with fresh cilantro or parsley.

2. Mahewu Bread: Mahewu bread is a delightful and hearty loaf that incorporates the distinctive taste of mahewu. It is often enjoyed as a quick breakfast or snack, either on its own or spread with butter or jam. Here's a simple recipe:

Ingredients:

- 2 cups of self-rising flour

- 1 cup of mahewu

- 2 tablespoons of sugar

- 2 tablespoons of melted butter

- 1 egg, beaten

- ½ cup of milk

Instructions:

1. Preheat your oven to 180°C (350°F) and grease a loaf pan.

2. In a mixing bowl, combine the self-rising flour and sugar.

3. In a separate bowl, whisk together the mahewu, melted butter, beaten egg, and milk until well combined.

4. Slowly pour the mahewu mixture into the flour mixture, stirring gently until a thick batter forms.

5. Pour the batter into the greased loaf pan and smooth the top with a spatula.

6. Bake the bread for approximately 40-45 minutes, or until a toothpick inserted into the center comes out clean.

7. Allow the bread to cool in the pan for a few minutes before transferring it to a wire rack to cool completely.

These are just a couple of examples of the many dishes that utilize mahewu in Zimbabwe and other Southern African countries. With its unique flavor and nutritious characteristics, mahewu adds a touch of traditional authenticity to diverse culinary creations.

Chapter 14: Kefir- The origin and adaptation of kefir in Africa

Kefir, a fermented milk beverage with a rich history, has been consumed by various cultures for centuries. While its origins can be traced back to the Caucasus Mountains in Eurasia, it has also found its way to other parts of the world, including Africa. This chapter explores the journey of kefir, its adaptation in Africa, and the various implications of its introduction to the continent.

1. From Caucasus to Africa: Tracing the Origin of Kefir:

The Caucasus Mountains, home to a diverse range of cultures and traditional foods, served as the birthplace of kefir. Nomadic tribes residing in this region discovered the unique properties of kefir grains that ferment milk, creating a probiotic drink. Ancient stories and legends attribute the origin of kefir to a religious prophet who gifted the grains to the Caucasus people by divine means.

2. Advent of Kefir in Africa:

It is believed that kefir was introduced to Africa through trade routes connecting the Arab world with the Eastern European regions. Early connections between the Ottoman Empire and Africa facilitated the transfer of kefir grains to the continent. Over time, kefir gained popularity among local communities for its purported health benefits and refreshing taste.

3. Adapting Kefir to African Ingredients and Traditions:

Once kefir made its way into Africa, local populations began experimenting with different ingredients and techniques to adapt it to their palates and dietary habits. In regions like North Africa, camel or goat milk was used instead of cow's milk as a base for kefir, giving it a distinctive taste. Fruits such as dates and figs were also incorporated, further enriching the beverage.

4. Health Benefits of Kefir in Africa:

African communities quickly recognized the health benefits associated with consuming kefir. The probiotics present in kefir aided digestion, boosted the immune system, and improved overall gut health. Many traditional healers and herbalists incorporated kefir into their remedies, using it to address various ailments.

5. Sociocultural Significance of Kefir in Africa:

As kefir became an integral part of African culinary practices, it also acquired sociocultural significance. In some regions, kefir was consumed during special occasions, such as weddings or religious festivals, signifying abundance and hospitality. Stories and folklore celebrating the mystical origins of kefir contributed to its cultural importance.

6. Impact of Kefir Commercialization in Africa:

While kefir initially thrived as a locally-produced beverage, commercialization and industrialization had significant effects on its production and consumption patterns. Large-scale dairy industries capitalized on the popularity of kefir, leading to the mass production of kefir products that often deviated from traditional recipes and fermentation methods. This shift raised concerns about authenticity and quality.

7. The Future of Kefir in Africa:

Despite concerns surrounding commercialization, the future of kefir in Africa remains promising. Efforts are being made to revive traditional production methods and encourage local communities to take part in kefir production. Additionally, innovative approaches such as using non-dairy sources for fermentation, like coconut milk or soy milk, are widening the options available to those with dietary restrictions or preferences.

⚬

THE JOURNEY OF KEFIR from the Caucasus Mountains to Africa is a testament to the cultural exchange and adaptation of food traditions. The integration of kefir into African cuisine has not only added a unique flavor, but it has also contributed to the health and well-being of communities across the continent. Embracing the heritage and time-honored production techniques can ensure that kefir continues to enrich the tastes and traditions of Africa for generations to come.

- The ingredients and methods of making kefir from fermented milk

Kefir is a traditional fermented milk beverage that originated in the Caucasus region. It is made by introducing kefir grains, a combination of bacteria and yeast, into fresh milk. The grains ferment the milk, resulting in a creamy and tangy drink that is packed with probiotics and nutrients.

To make kefir, you will need the following ingredients:

- Kefir grains: These can be purchased from health food stores or obtained from someone who already makes kefir. They are small, gelatinous clusters that resemble cauliflower florets.

- Milk: Any type of milk can be used to make kefir, including cow's milk, goat's milk, or plant-based alternatives such as coconut or almond milk. It is best to use full-fat milk as it provides a richer and creamier texture.

Here is the step-by-step process of making kefir:

1. Add the kefir grains to a clean glass jar or container.

2. Pour fresh milk over the grains until the container is about ¾ full.

3. Stir gently with a non-metal spoon to ensure the grains are evenly distributed throughout the milk.

4. Cover the jar with a cloth or a loose-fitting lid. This is important as kefir fermentation produces carbon dioxide, and the container needs to allow gases to escape.

5. Let the mixture sit at room temperature away from direct sunlight for approximately 24-48 hours. The fermentation time may vary depending on the ambient temperature and how tangy you prefer your kefir. The longer the fermentation, the tangier and the thicker the kefir will become.

6. After the desired fermentation time, strain the kefir into another clean container, separating the grains from the liquid. You can use a plastic or wooden mesh strainer to avoid damaging the grains.

7. The strained kefir is now ready to be consumed. You can refrigerate it for a few hours to cool it down or enjoy it as is.

8. Rinse the kefir grains with filtered water to remove any milk residue. They are now ready for another batch of kefir.

9. You can start the process again with the strained grains and repeat this cycle indefinitely.

It is important to note that kefir grains are living organisms, and they need to be cared for to ensure the longevity and the quality of your kefir. When you are not using them, they can be stored in a jar filled with milk in the refrigerator for up to a week.

Kefir is not only a delightful beverage but also a valuable source of probiotics and essential nutrients. Regular consumption of kefir may contribute to improved digestion and enhanced immune function. So why not give it a try and embark on this delicious and healthy journey of fermentation!

- The examples and recipes of dishes that use kefir in Africa

In Africa, kefir is not as widely consumed as in other parts of the world, but there are certainly some delicious dishes that showcase this cultured milk beverage. Kefir, known for its rich probiotics and tangy flavor, can be incorporated into dishes to add a unique and healthy twist. Here are a few examples and recipes of African dishes that use kefir:

1. Kefir Lassi:

Lassi is a popular yogurt-based drink in India, but a similar variation can be made using kefir. To make a kefir lassi, blend kefir with your choice of fruits, such as mango or berries, and add a little honey or sugar for sweetness. This refreshing drink is perfect for summers in Africa, providing a cool and nutritious experience.

Ingredients:

- 1 cup kefir

- 1 ripe mango, peeled and cubed (or any other fruit)

- 1 tablespoon honey (optional)

- Ice cubes (optional)

Instructions:

1. In a blender, combine kefir, mango, honey, and ice cubes (if using).

2. Blend until smooth and frothy.

3. Pour into glasses and serve chilled.

2. Kefir Pancakes:

Add a healthy twist to traditional African pancakes by using kefir instead of regular milk. Kefir enhances the fluffiness and adds a beautiful tang to the pancakes. Serve them with fresh fruit, honey, or syrup for a wholesome breakfast or snack option.

Ingredients:

- 1 cup all-purpose flour

- 1 tablespoon sugar

- 1 teaspoon baking powder

- 1/2 teaspoon baking soda

- 1/4 teaspoon salt

- 1 cup kefir

- 1 large egg

- 1 tablespoon melted butter (optional)

- Cooking oil or butter for frying

Instructions:

1. In a mixing bowl, whisk together flour, sugar, baking powder, baking soda, and salt.

2. In a separate bowl, whisk kefir, egg, and melted butter (if using).

3. Pour the wet ingredients into the dry ingredients and stir until just combined.

4. Heat a non-stick frying pan or griddle over medium heat and lightly grease with oil or butter.

5. Pour 1/4 cup of batter onto the hot pan for each pancake.

6. Cook until bubbles form on the surface, then flip and cook the other side until golden brown.

7. Repeat with the remaining batter and serve warm with your choice of toppings.

3. Kefir Veggie Dip:

Use kefir as a base in a creamy vegetable dip to enjoy with fresh cut vegetables or as a spread for sandwiches and wraps. This dip is packed with probiotics and can be made more flavorful by adding herbs and spices of your choice.

Ingredients:

- 1 cup kefir

- 1/4 cup chopped cucumber

- 1/4 cup finely chopped bell peppers (any color)

- 1 tablespoon finely chopped fresh herbs (such as mint, cilantro, or dill)

- 1/2 teaspoon garlic powder

- Salt and pepper to taste

Instructions:

1. In a mixing bowl, combine kefir, chopped cucumber, bell peppers, and fresh herbs.

2. Stir in garlic powder, salt, and pepper to taste.

3. Mix well until all ingredients are incorporated.

4. Serve with fresh vegetables or as a spread for sandwiches and wraps.

These are just a few examples of how kefir can be incorporated into African dishes. Experimenting with kefir in various recipes can provide new flavors and a healthier twist to traditional African cuisine. So don't hesitate to get creative and introduce the goodness of kefir into your meals!

Chapter 15: Kimchi- The origin and adaptation of kimchi in Africa

Kimchi, a traditional Korean dish made from fermented vegetables, has gained international popularity in recent years. While it remains most closely associated with Korean cuisine, its versatility and health benefits have led to its introduction and adaptation in various parts of the world. This chapter explores the origin and subsequent adaptation of kimchi specifically in Africa, unveiling the unique ways in which this beloved dish found its place in a continent known for its own diverse culinary traditions.

The Historical Journey of Kimchi:

Originally traced back to the 7th century, kimchi was developed as a means to preserve vegetables during the harsh Korean winters. It evolved over time, incorporating new ingredients and techniques, becoming an integral part of Korean culture. With the Korean diaspora spreading across the globe, kimchi traveled new horizons and embraced innovative adaptations to align with local tastes and availability of ingredients.

The Arrival of Kimchi in Africa:

The introduction of kimchi in Africa can be credited to Korean immigrants who arrived in various African countries during the mid-20th century. As these individuals brought with them their culinary traditions, kimchi found a foothold in African communities, being prepared and shared among newly settled Korean communities. However, its popularity didn't stop there.

Discovering Local Ingredients:

One of the significant ways kimchi has adapted in Africa is through the incorporation of local ingredients. Africa's fertile lands provide an abundance of vegetables that have seamlessly integrated into traditional kimchi recipes. Local vegetables such as okra, cassava leaves, and moringa have replaced conventional Korean favorites like napa cabbage, radishes, and chili peppers. This ingenious adaptation has not only made kimchi more accessible but has added a distinct African flair to the dish.

Fermentation Techniques:

Kimchi owes its unique tangy flavor to the process of lacto-fermentation, which occurs when the vegetables are soaked in a brine solution. African communities have developed their own fermentation techniques based on traditional methods and climate conditions. For example, in hotter regions, shorter fermentation periods are employed, resulting in milder and less sour kimchi. African spices and seasoning have also found their way into the fermenting process, further contributing to the evolution of kimchi in Africa.

Incorporation into Local Cuisine:

As kimchi became more prevalent in African countries, it gradually seeped into the local culinary traditions. In South Africa, the popular street food "bunny chow" saw creative variations emerging, incorporating kimchi for an interplay of spicy and tangy flavors. In Nigeria, kimchi was fused with local salsa to create a vibrant accompaniment to traditional rice dishes. The fusion of alma, a traditional Egyptian pickled vegetable dish, with kimchi has also resulted in delightful recipes bridging the gap between African and Korean cuisines.

Health Benefits and Culinary Interest:

Similar to other parts of the world, Africans have embraced kimchi not only for its unique taste but also for its health benefits. Fermented foods, including kimchi, contain probiotics that promote gut health and offer favorable effects on overall well-being. Africans' growing interest in health-conscious cooking has provided an additional impetus for the popularity of this Korean delicacy in a continent laden with rich culinary heritage.

⊷⊶

KIMCHI, ONCE A PRESERVED Korean dish, has found its place in Africa through the adaptation of local ingredients, fermentation techniques, and incorporation into traditional African cuisines. The fusion of Korean and African flavors and textures has resulted in a unique culinary phenomenon, showcasing the perpetual evolution of food traditions. The journey of kimchi in Africa serves as a testament to the enduring allure of food and its timeless ability to adapt, transcend borders, and bring diverse communities together.

- The ingredients and methods of making kimchi from fermented cabbage

Kimchi is a traditional Korean dish that has gained popularity all over the world for its unique taste and health benefits. Made primarily from fermented cabbage and spices, kimchi adds a burst of flavor to any meal. In this article, we will explore the ingredients and methods used to make this delicious Korean staple.

The main ingredient in kimchi is Napa cabbage, a type of Chinese cabbage that is traditionally used for making this fermented dish. Napa cabbage has a mild and sweet taste, making it the perfect base for creating the tangy flavors of kimchi. Apart from Napa cabbage, other vegetables such as radishes and green onions are also added to enhance the overall taste and texture of the dish.

To make kimchi, the cabbage is first washed and sliced into bite-sized pieces. It is then salted and left to sit for a few hours in order to remove excess water and to give it a crisp texture. After the cabbage has been salted, it is rinsed thoroughly to remove any remaining salt and then drained.

The next step is to create the marinade that will give kimchi its distinctive taste. The marinade is made by combining ingredients such as Korean red pepper flakes, ginger, garlic, fish sauce, soy sauce, and sugar. These ingredients are mixed together to create a paste-like consistency, which is then added to the drained cabbage along with the other vegetables.

Once all the ingredients are mixed together, they are packed tightly into glass jars or other airtight containers. The key to successful fermentation is making sure that the kimchi is submerged in its own liquid, as this helps to create an anaerobic environment necessary for fermentation. The fermentation process can take anywhere from a few days to a few weeks, depending on the desired level of sourness and the ambient temperature.

During the fermentation process, various microorganisms, including lactic acid bacteria, begin to break down the sugars present in the vegetables, producing lactic acid. This lactic acid gives kimchi its tangy flavor as well as its characteristic probiotic properties, which are known for promoting digestive health. Additionally, fermentation enhances the umami flavors and transforms the texture of the vegetables, making them softer and more flavorful.

Once kimchi has reached the desired level of fermentation, it is refrigerated to slow down the process. Kimchi can be consumed immediately, but many people prefer to let it age in the refrigerator for a few weeks before consuming, as this further enhances the flavors.

Now that you know the ingredients and methods used to make kimchi, you can try your hand at making this delicious and healthy dish at home. Whether you enjoy it on its own as a side dish, or use it to add extra flavor to soups, stews, or stir-fries, kimchi is a versatile and flavorful addition to any meal. So go ahead, grab some cabbage, gather your spices, and get ready to embark on your kimchi-making adventure.

- The examples and recipes of dishes that use kimchi in Africa

Exploring the Use of Kimchi in African Cuisine: Examples and Recipes

KIMCHI, THE TRADITIONAL Korean fermented side dish, has gained popularity around the world due to its unique and tangy flavor. Although primarily associated with Korean cuisine, kimchi has made its way to various parts of the globe, including Africa. In this article, we will delve into the fascinating world of kimchi-infused African dishes. We will explore the unexpected ways in which this traditional Korean delicacy has found its place in African culinary landscapes and provide you with some inspiring recipes that combine the best of both worlds.

1. Kimchi Jollof Rice:

One popular African dish that has embraced the flavors of kimchi is Jollof Rice, a staple in West African cuisine. Jollof Rice is a one-pot rice dish typically cooked with tomatoes, spices, and various meats or vegetables. The addition of kimchi brings a new dimension of flavor, adding a tangy and umami kick to the already delicious rice dish. To prepare this fusion delight, caramelize onions, garlic, and ginger, then add chopped kimchi and fry for a few minutes. Incorporate cooked rice, tomato paste, spices, and seasoning. Simmer until all the flavors meld together, and enjoy the unique taste of Kimchi Jollof Rice!

2. Kimchi Bunny Chow:

Bunny Chow hails from South Africa, with its roots in the Indian community. Traditionally, Bunny Chow consists of a hollowed-out loaf of bread filled with curry. Add a twist to this beloved dish by infusing it with the flavors of kimchi. Prepare a kimchi curry using your preferred meat or vegetables with aromatic masalas and spices. Once the curry is cooked, take a loaf of bread and scoop out some of the inside, creating a hollow space. Fill this cavity with the kimchi curry, ensuring it soaks into the bread, and ensuring every bite is a harmonious blend of African and Korean flavors.

3. Kimchi and Bobotie Samosas:

Samosas, triangular pastries stuffed with savory fillings, are popular in different parts of Africa. Give the classic samosa an innovative touch by incorporating kimchi and Bobotie, a spiced minced-meat dish from South Africa. Prepare the Bobotie filling (typically made with minced meat, onions, spices, and raisins), along with chopped kimchi. Mix these ingredients together to form a rich and flavorsome stuffing. Wrap the filling in samosa wrappers, fry until golden brown, and serve with your favorite dipping sauce. These fusion samosas bring together the distinct flavors of kimchi and Bobotie, taking your taste buds on an unforgettable journey.

⎯⎯⎯◉⎯⎯⎯

AS THE CULINARY WORLD becomes more interconnected, the fusion of flavors from different cuisines is becoming a delightful norm. Kimchi, while geographically distant from Africa, has managed to seamlessly marry with a range of African dishes, introducing new dimensions and tastes. Inspired by Korean and African ingredients, our examples and recipes demonstrate just a few of the ways kimchi has made its flavorful mark on African cuisine. So, next time you're in the mood for something unique and adventurous, give one of these fusion recipes a try and experience the delicious marriage of Korean and African flavors!

Chapter 16: Sauerkraut- The origin and adaptation of sauerkraut in Africa

The Global Reach of Sauerkraut

Sauerkraut, the fermented cabbage dish originating in Eastern Europe, has gained popularity around the world due to its unique tangy taste and numerous health benefits. While it is often associated with European cuisine, sauerkraut has also found its way into other regions, including Africa. In this chapter, we will explore the captivating journey of sauerkraut's origin and how it has been adapted and integrated into the diverse culinary traditions of Africa.

1. Ancient Beginnings and Migration

The origins of sauerkraut trace back thousands of years to ancient China and Mesopotamia, where people discovered the concept of fermenting cabbage. The process was later adopted and refined by the Romans and eventually spread across Europe during invasions and trade routes.

2. Colonial Influence

The arrival of European colonizers in Africa during the 15th century introduced the continent to various aspects of European culture, including food and culinary practices. Sauerkraut was one such food that found its way onto colonial tables, initially served to European settlers and military establishments.

3. Integration into Local Cuisine

Over time, sauerkraut underwent a fascinating transformation as it merged with the local culinary traditions of African nations. This integration was largely driven by the African people's adaptability and resourcefulness, as well as their desire to incorporate new flavors into their diets.

4. Nigerian Sauerkraut- "Ekoko"

In Nigeria, sauerkraut is known as "ekoko" and has become a popular addition to local dishes. The traditional Nigerian method involves fermenting shredded cabbage with palm oil, ginger, and various spices. This gives the sauerkraut a distinctively spicier and richer flavor compared to its European counterpart.

5. South African Sauerkraut- "Mallemolen"

In South Africa, sauerkraut has assimilated into the local cuisine through a dish called "mallemolen." To create mallemolen, cabbage is fermented with indigenous ingredients such as rooibos tea, honeybush, and traditional African spices. The result is a vibrant sauerkraut with a unique flavor profile that complements various South African dishes.

6. Ethiopian Sauerkraut- "Tere sega"

In Ethiopia, sauerkraut, or "tere sega," plays a prominent role in traditional Ethiopian cuisine. Here, shredded cabbage is fermented with spices known as "berbere," a traditional Ethiopian spice blend featuring an array of chilies, herbs, and spices. This infusion of flavors creates a fiery sauerkraut that is revered for its

7. The Health Benefits of African Sauerkraut

Besides its flavorful taste, African sauerkraut offers numerous health benefits. The fermentation process enhances its nutritional value, making it rich in probiotics and enzymes that aid digestion, boost the immune system, and improve gut health. Additionally, it provides a healthy source of dietary fiber, vitamins C and K, and other essential nutrients.

Sauerkraut's Resilience and Continual Evolution

The journey of sauerkraut in Africa showcases the versatility and adaptability of this ancient fermented dish. Through centuries of migration, colonization, and the integration of local culinary traditions, sauerkraut has found a home in African cuisine. It has been transformed, adding unique African flavors and adapting to local tastes. African sauerkraut serves as a testament to the enduring nature of food, its ability to travel across borders, and the remarkable evolution it undergoes in diverse cultural settings.

- The ingredients and methods of making sauerkraut from fermented cabbage

Sauerkraut, a staple in many cuisines around the world, is a traditional dish made from fermented cabbage. The tangy and slightly sour flavor of sauerkraut adds depth and complexity to various dishes, making it a beloved ingredient among food enthusiasts. In this article, we will delve into the ingredients and methods used to make this delectable fermented condiment.

Ingredients:

- Cabbage: The star ingredient of sauerkraut is cabbage. Choose fresh and firm heads of cabbage, preferably organic, to achieve the best results. You can use green or red cabbage, or a combination of the two, depending on your preference.

- Salt: Salt plays a crucial role in the fermentation process, as it assists in breaking down the natural sugars of the cabbage and prevents the growth of harmful bacteria. It is recommended to use pickling or kosher salt since they lack additives such as iodine or anti-caking agents.

Optional Ingredients:

- Caraway Seeds: To add an aromatic note to your sauerkraut, you can include a teaspoon or more of caraway seeds. These seeds contribute a distinct flavor profile and complement the natural taste of the fermentation process.

- Juniper Berries: For a unique twist, consider adding a few juniper berries. These berries provide a subtle piney flavor that pairs exceptionally well with the cabbage.

Methods:

1. Prepare the Cabbage:

Start by removing the outer leaves of the cabbage heads. Rinse the cabbage under cold water and pat it dry. You can chop the cabbage finely with a sharp knife or use a mandoline or food processor for a finer consistency. Remember to remove the core and tough veins of the cabbage before proceeding.

2. Add Salt:

Place the chopped or shredded cabbage in a large mixing bowl. Sprinkle a couple of tablespoons of salt over the cabbage, adding more if needed. The exact amount of salt depends on the quantity of cabbage and personal taste preferences. Toss the cabbage to distribute the salt evenly and let it rest for about 10-15 minutes. During this time, the salt extracts moisture from the cabbage, aiding in the fermentation process.

3. Massage and Ferment:

After the cabbage has rested, start massaging it with your hands. The pressure applied during massaging helps to further release water from the cabbage, creating its own brine. The brine acts as a protective layer, preventing the growth of undesirable bacteria.

Once the cabbage is evenly moist and has reduced in volume, transfer it to a fermentation vessel. This could be a fermentation crock or a mason jar with an airtight seal. Whichever vessel you choose, remember to press down the cabbage, ensuring it is completely submerged in its brine. This minimizes contact with air and encourages anaerobic fermentation.

4. Weighing It Down:

To keep the cabbage fully submerged, you can use weights or a cabbage leaf as a cover to maintain proper anaerobic conditions. Cover the vessel but leave it slightly loose to allow any gases produced during fermentation to escape.

5. Fermentation Time:

Now comes the waiting game. Allow the cabbage to ferment at room temperature, preferably somewhere between 60-70°F (15-21°C). Fermentation can take anywhere from a few days to several weeks, depending on the taste and texture you desire. Taste the sauerkraut after a few days to monitor its progress. Once it has reached the desired level of tanginess, you can transfer it to the refrigerator to slow down fermentation and preserve its flavor.

Remember to check the sauerkraut occasionally during the fermentation process to ensure there is no mold or other signs of spoilage. If you observe any such signs, it is advisable to discard the entire batch.

After refrigerating, sauerkraut can be enjoyed for several months, intensifying in flavor over time. It works wonderfully as a side dish, topping for sausages or sandwiches, or even as an ingredient in various recipes. The versatility of sauerkraut makes it a valuable addition to any culinary repertoire.

In conclusion, sauerkraut's delightful taste and numerous health benefits are a product of simple ingredients and a straightforward fermentation process. Try making your own sauerkraut and explore the rich and diverse world of fermented foods.

- The examples and recipes of dishes that use sauerkraut in Africa

While sauerkraut might not be commonly associated with African cuisine, it is indeed used in a few dishes across the continent. Influences from European colonization and the more recent globalization have introduced sauerkraut as an ingredient in certain regions. Here are a few examples and recipes of dishes that incorporate sauerkraut in Africa:

1. Bunny Chow (South Africa):

Bunny Chow is a popular street food originating from the Indian community in Durban, South Africa. It consists of a hollowed-out loaf of bread filled with a flavorful curry. In some variations, sauerkraut is added to the curry to enhance its tangy taste and add a unique twist to the dish.

Recipe:

- Heat oil in a pan and sauté finely chopped onions until golden brown.

- Add garlic, ginger, and curry powder to the onions and sauté for a minute or two.

- Throw in your choice of vegetables, such as potatoes, carrots, and bell peppers, and cook until slightly tender.

- Pour in a can of sauerkraut along with its juice and cook for a few more minutes.

- Add some water or vegetable broth to achieve the desired consistency.

- Serve the sauerkraut curry inside a hollowed-out loaf of bread and garnish with fresh cilantro.

2. Senegalese Thieboudienne (Senegal):

Thieboudienne is the national dish of Senegal and is known for its savory flavor and vibrant presentation. Typically, sauerkraut is used in this dish as a condiment to balance the richness of flavors from the braised fish and vegetables.

Recipe:

- Marinate pieces of bone-in fish (like sea bass or red snapper) in a blend of lemon juice, garlic, chili powder, and thyme for at least 30 minutes.

- In a large pot, heat oil and brown the fish on both sides. Remove and set aside.

- In the same pot, sauté diced onions, bell peppers, and tomatoes until softened.

- Add water, tomato paste, and a selection of vegetables like carrots, cabbage, eggplant, and chayote.

- Season with salt, black pepper, cayenne pepper, and Maggi seasoning cubes to taste.

- Simmer until the vegetables are tender and the flavors have melded together.

- Serve the Thieboudienne, placing a spoonful of sauerkraut on top of each portion.

3. Makbouba (Tunisia):

Makbouba is a combination of cooked farina (couscous) and an assortment of vegetables and meat. In this North African dish, sauerkraut is often used to add a delightful zing to the mixture of flavors.

Recipe:

- Sauté diced onions, garlic, and your choice of meat (like lamb or chicken) until browned.

- Add spices such as cumin, turmeric, cinnamon, and chili flakes to the mixture.

- Pour in water or chicken broth and bring to a simmer.

- Add chopped vegetables like carrots, peas, and diced tomatoes.

- Once the vegetables are cooked, stir in cooked farina and a can of sauerkraut, including the juices.

- Allow all the flavors to blend together for a few minutes before serving.

While the use of sauerkraut in African cuisine might not be as widespread as in European dishes, these examples demonstrate how it can contribute a unique twist and flavor to traditional African recipes.

Chapter 17: Yogurt- The origin and adaptation of yogurt in Africa

Yogurt is a fermented dairy product that has been consumed for centuries worldwide. It has gained popularity due to its unique taste, nutritional benefits, and its ability to improve overall gut health. While yogurt is often associated with European countries, its origin can be traced back to ancient civilizations such as those in Africa. In this chapter, we will explore the fascinating journey of yogurt in Africa, from its inception to its adaptation in diverse African cultures.

An Ancient Secret: The Birth of Yogurt in Africa

Africa, with its rich history and diverse communities, has played a significant role in the development of this cherished food. The exact origin of yogurt in Africa is still debated among historians, but evidence suggests that it dates back thousands of years. Ancient African tribes, such as the Maasai in East Africa and the Fulani in West Africa, have been making and consuming yogurt for generations.

Traditional Yogurt-Making Techniques: A Unique Process

In Africa, yogurt is traditionally made from milk obtained from various animals, including cattle, goats, and camels. The milk is heated and then cooled to activate the fermentation process, initiated by natural bacteria naturally present in the milk. This natural fermentation process transforms milk sugars (lactose) into lactic acid, which gives yogurt its distinct tangy flavor and thick texture.

Local Ingredients: The African Twist

A notable feature of yogurt in Africa is the use of indigenous ingredients that add a unique twist to this beloved food. In some regions, yogurt is flavored with local fruits such as baobab, guava, or papaya, resulting in vibrant and refreshing flavors. In other areas, herbs and spices like mint, cinnamon, or ginger are added to yogurt, giving it an aromatic and multi-dimensional taste.

Health Benefits of African Yogurt: Enhancing Well-Being

African yogurt's long-standing tradition has contributed to a rich knowledge of its health benefits. The natural probiotics found in yogurt help to promote a healthy digestive system, reduce bloating, and enhance nutrient absorption. Additionally, the high protein content in yogurt is vital for muscle development and repair. The adaptation of yogurt in Africa has not only preserved ancient recipes but also unlocked a world of nutritional advantages.

Yogurt as a Cultural Symbol: Celebrating Diversity

Today, yogurt has become deeply ingrained in African regional cultures, reflecting the continent's diverse traditions. In East Africa, yogurt is often considered a symbol of hospitality and is served as a welcoming drink to guests. In some West African countries, yogurt is a cherished component of festive feasts and special occasions. The ability of yogurt to adapt and gain cultural symbolism demonstrates the rich interconnectedness between food and regional identity.

Yogurt's Economic Impact: Empowering African Dairy Farmers

The production and consumption of yogurt in Africa have provided significant economic opportunities for local dairy farmers and small-scale entrepreneurial ventures. The increasing demand for yogurt has created a market niche, enabling dairy farmers to develop sustainable businesses. This economic empowerment goes even further by helping to alleviate poverty and generate local employment in different regions across Africa.

The Journey of Yogurt in Africa

From its mysterious origins to its current adaptation in diverse African cultures, yogurt has played an essential role in the continent's culinary heritage. The historical knowledge and traditional techniques associated with yogurt-making in Africa contribute to its unique taste, health benefits, and economic impact. By embracing its rich past, Africa continues to pave the way for the future of yogurt, ensuring that this ancient wonder will continue to delight taste buds, enhance well-being, and empower communities for generations to come.

Word count: 600

- The ingredients and methods of making yogurt from fermented milk

Yogurt is a versatile and popular dairy product that is enjoyed by many people around the world. It is not only delicious but also packed with essential nutrients and beneficial bacteria that promote good gut health. Have you ever wondered how yogurt is made from fermented milk? Let's dive into the fascinating world of yogurt production, exploring the ingredients and methods involved in bringing this delightful treat to our tables.

The primary ingredient in yogurt is milk, which can come from various sources, such as cow, goat, sheep, or even buffalo. It is important to use high-quality milk as the fermenting process will highlight the characteristics of the milk used. To create yogurt, you will also need a starter culture. This consists of live bacteria, specifically Lactobacillus bulgaricus and Streptococcus thermophilus, which are responsible for fermenting the milk and transforming it into yogurt.

The process of making yogurt starts by heating the milk to the desired temperature. This step serves two purposes: to kill any harmful bacteria present in the milk and to denature the proteins, which promotes a thicker yogurt consistency. The temperature can range between 180°F to 200°F (82°C to 93°C), depending on the desired outcome. After heating, the milk must be cooled down to approximately 110°F to 115°F (43°C to 46°C) before proceeding.

Once the milk has reached the appropriate temperature, the starter culture is added. The starter culture is usually obtained from a previously made batch of yogurt, but it can also be purchased in a powdered form. The live bacteria present in the culture will gradually multiply and ferment the lactose sugar naturally occurring in the milk. This fermentation process produces lactic acid, which imparts the tangy taste to the yogurt and causes the milk proteins to curdle, transforming the milk into a creamy, thick texture.

Maintaining the ideal temperature is crucial during fermentation. Wrapping the container with a warm towel or placing it in a yogurt maker helps create an ideal environment for the bacteria to flourish. The fermentation process can take anywhere from 4 to 12 hours, depending on the desired level of tanginess and thickness. The longer the yogurt is left to ferment, the tangier and firmer it becomes.

After the required fermentation period, the yogurt should be cooled down in the refrigerator to halt the bacterial activity. This chilling process allows the flavors to develop further, resulting in a smoother and more delightful yogurt. Once cooled, the yogurt is ready to be enjoyed on its own or customized with various toppings like fresh fruits, honey, granola, or nuts.

It is noteworthy that commercially produced yogurt often goes through additional steps to optimize taste, texture, and shelf life. These might include stabilizers, sweeteners, and flavorings, depending on the brand and type of yogurt being produced. However, for those looking to experience the true taste and health benefits of yogurt, making it at home using the traditional method is a rewarding and simple process.

Yogurt is not only a delectable treat but also a nutritious addition to any diet. Through the fermentation of milk with live bacterial cultures, yogurt provides essential nutrients, including protein, calcium, and various vitamins and minerals. Additionally, the beneficial bacteria found in yogurt, known as probiotics, help maintain a healthy digestive system and support overall well-being.

In conclusion, making yogurt from fermented milk requires few ingredients and straightforward techniques. The orchestration of live bacteria, temperature control, and the right fermentation time is key to achieving delicious, creamy, and healthy yogurt. Whether enjoyed on its own or used as an ingredient in a variety of dishes, yogurt continues to be a delightful and versatile addition to our meals. So why not venture into your kitchen and try making your own yogurt from fermented milk?

- The examples and recipes of dishes that use yogurt in Africa

Africa is a continent known for its rich and diverse cuisine, and one ingredient that is commonly used in various dishes is yogurt. Also known as "maziwa lala" in Swahili and "amasi" in Zulu, yogurt is a creamy and tangy dairy product that has been a part of African culinary traditions for centuries. From savory stews to refreshing beverages, yogurt is a versatile ingredient that adds a unique flavor and texture to African dishes. Let's explore some examples and recipes that showcase the delicious use of yogurt in African cuisine.

1. Mashed Plantains with Spiced Yogurt: A popular dish in West Africa, mashed plantains are cooked until soft and then mashed with spices such as ginger, garlic, and cayenne pepper. These flavorful mashed plantains are often served with a dollop of spiced yogurt, made by mixing plain yogurt with ground cinnamon, cardamom, and a touch of honey. The creamy and tangy yogurt complements the sweet and spiced plantains, creating a delectable balance of flavors.

2. Yoghurt Chicken Curry: A classic East African dish, yoghurt chicken curry is a flavorful and aromatic curry that brings together tender chicken and a yogurt-based sauce. The chicken is marinated with yogurt, along with a blend of spices such as turmeric, coriander, cumin, and paprika. The marinated chicken is then simmered in a tomato and yogurt sauce until tender and infused with all the spices. The result is a creamy, luscious curry bursting with the flavors of Africa.

3. Yogurt Jollof Rice: Jollof rice is a beloved West African dish that is typically made with rice, tomatoes, onions, and a medley of spices. To give it a unique twist, yogurt can be added to the jollof rice, adding a velvety richness to the dish. The yogurt not only enhances the creaminess of the rice but also helps balance out the heat from the spicy flavors. It adds a tangy undertone that elevates the taste of this already flavorful African staple.

4. Aiyeko: A refreshing Tanzanian beverage, Aiyeko is made by blending fresh mangoes, yogurt, and a touch of honey. This creamy drink offers a delightful combination of the sweetness from the mangoes and the tanginess from the yogurt. It is then chilled and served over ice, making it a perfect thirst quencher on hot summer days. The addition of yogurt not only enhances the texture of this drink but also provides a probiotic boost to support a healthy digestive system.

These are just a few examples of the diverse range of dishes that utilize yogurt in African cuisine. Whether it's in main courses, side dishes, or even desserts, yogurt plays a significant role in adding depth and flavor to the culinary traditions across the continent. Its creamy texture and tangy taste are a wonderful addition to a vast array of ingredients, creating a harmonious blend of flavors that celebrates the vibrancy and cultural heritage of Africa.

Chapter 18: Kombucha- The origin and adaptation of kombucha in Africa

Kombucha, a fermented tea beverage known for its tangy flavor and numerous health benefits, has been gaining popularity worldwide in recent years. While its precise origin remains a subject of debate, evidence suggests that kombucha originated in China around 220 BCE during the Qin Dynasty. However, what many people may not know is that kombucha has also found its place in Africa, where it has adapted and taken on its unique characteristics.

Africa has a rich history of traditional fermented beverages, and kombucha has seamlessly integrated into this cultural tapestry. It is believed that kombucha was introduced to Africa through trade routes, particularly during interactions between the indigenous African tribes and Arab traders along the east coast of the continent. As these traders brought along various goods, including different types of tea, it is thought that kombucha cultures were introduced to African communities.

Traditionally, African cultures have a deep-rooted reliance on natural fermentation processes for the preservation of foods and the creation of unique flavors. Fermented beverages, in particular, have been an integral part of African culinary traditions for centuries, offering not only refreshment but also numerous health benefits. Thus, kombucha found a natural place within the African cultural landscape, aligning with existing fermentation practices and beliefs.

However, like many food and beverages that migrate between regions, kombucha quickly began to integrate African ingredients and techniques into its production. One notable adaptation is the inclusion of indigenous African medicinal herbs, which are added to the kombucha brew to enhance its health properties. These herbs, such as Rooibos, a South African indigenous shrub known for its antioxidant and anti-inflammatory properties, further elevate kombucha's already well-known health benefits.

Furthermore, African adaptations of kombucha have also extended to the choice of tea base used for brewing. While the original Chinese kombucha typically used green or black tea, African kombucha often incorporates locally available teas like hibiscus and honeybush. This infusion of local flavors and ingredients has resulted in uniquely African kombucha varieties that reflect the continent's diverse cultural heritage.

In addition to its adaptation to local ingredients, kombucha in Africa has also experienced a revival through artisanal production methods. Many small-scale producers have embraced kombucha as a means of promoting sustainable livelihoods and preserving traditional knowledge. These producers prioritize organic farming practices and source their tea leaves from local tea plantations, supporting local economies and sustainable agricultural practices.

Beyond its culinary importance and cultural significance, kombucha in Africa has also become a focal point for entrepreneurship and community development. Social enterprises focused on kombucha production have emerged across the continent, empowering women and marginalized communities by providing them with training and economic opportunities. These enterprises not only contribute to economic growth but also foster a sense of pride and ownership of local cultural heritage.

In summary, the origin and adaptation of kombucha in Africa showcase the cultural fluidity and adaptability of fermented beverages. Kombucha seamlessly integrated into African fermentation practices, incorporating local ingredients and medicinal herbs to create unique and health-enhancing variations. By embracing kombucha, African communities have not only expanded their beverage choices but also empowered themselves economically and preserved their cultural traditions. The story of kombucha in Africa exemplifies how culinary practices can evolve, adapt, and thrive when embraced and enriched by different cultures.

- The ingredients and methods of making kombucha from fermented tea

Kombucha, a slightly effervescent drink made from fermented tea, has gained popularity in recent years due to its potential health benefits and delightful taste. If you are intrigued by this ancient elixir, let's delve into the ingredients and methods required to craft your own kombucha at home.

First and foremost, you will need a SCOBY (Symbiotic Culture of Bacteria and Yeast) to initiate fermentation. A SCOBY resembles a slimy pancake or jellyfish-like organism and acts as the primary fermenting agent. It can be obtained by a generous donation from someone who already brews kombucha or purchased online or at local health food stores.

Next, gather the following ingredients:

1. Tea: Black and green teas are commonly used as the base for kombucha. Avoid flavoured or herbal teas, as they may contain oils or ingredients that can hinder fermentation. Opt for loose tea or tea bags, noting that one tea bag or two teaspoons of loose tea per 500ml (16 ounces) of water is a suitable ratio.

2. Sugar: Fermentation requires sugar as a food source for SCOBY. Organic white sugar is often used, but other options like cane sugar can work as well. Avoid alternative sweeteners, as they do not provide appropriate nutrition for fermentation.

3. Water: Use filtered or spring water to avoid any chlorine or chemicals that may hinder fermentation. Tap water can also be used, but let it sit uncovered overnight to allow chlorine to dissipate.

Once you have gathered these ingredients, you are ready to embark on the following process:

1. Boil water: Bring a large pot of water to a rolling boil. The amount of water required depends on how much kombucha you intend to brew.

2. Steep tea: Turn off the heat and add the appropriate amount of tea leaves or tea bags to the hot water. Let it steep for around 10-15 minutes, or according to the instructions on the tea packaging.

3. Add sugar: Measure the desired amount of sugar specified in your recipe and stir it into the tea until completely dissolved. Wait for the sweetened tea to cool down to room temperature.

4. Transfer to fermenting vessel: Pour the cooled tea into a clean, sterilized glass jar or ceramic crock, leaving some headspace for SCOBY growth. Make sure to use non-metallic utensils and vessels, as metal can interfere with fermentation.

5. Add SCOBY and starter liquid: Place the SCOBY gently into the container, with the smooth side facing up. Add around 10-15% starter liquid, which is the liquid from a previous batch of kombucha or store-bought plain kombucha. This starter liquid helps provide an acidic environment necessary for fermentation.

6. Cover and ferment: Secure a breathable cover on top of the container to prevent contamination while allowing airflow. A tightly woven cloth or a coffee filter secured with a rubber band works well. Store the jar in a warm, dark place, away from direct sunlight. Fermentation typically takes 7-14 days, but taste it periodically to find your desired level of sweetness and acidity.

7. Harvest and bottle: With a clean spoon, gently lift out the SCOBY and set it aside along with some of the starter liquid, ready for your next batch. Pour the fermented kombucha through a mesh strainer into clean glass bottles, discarding any sediment or unwanted particles.

8. Carbonation (optional): If you prefer fizzy kombucha, seal the bottles tightly with caps or lids and let them sit at room temperature for 1-2 days. This secondary fermentation will allow the kombucha to develop carbonation. Be cautious during this process to prevent bottle explosions caused by excessive carbonation.

9. Refrigerate and enjoy: After the secondary fermentation, transfer the bottles to the refrigerator to halt fermentation and develop flavor. Serve your homemade kombucha chilled, and savor the fascinating tangy, slightly vinegary taste!

Remember, making kombucha involves patience, experimentation, and careful attention to maintain cleanliness throughout the process. Don't be afraid to try different teas and flavors to customize your kombucha to suit your preferences. So, roll up your sleeves, embrace the art of fermentation, and enjoy your journey into the intriguing world of homemade kombucha!

- The examples and recipes of dishes that use kombucha in Africa

Exploring Kombucha Infused Dishes in African Culinary Traditions: Recipes and Experiences

KOMBUCHA, A FERMENTED tea beverage with numerous health benefits, has gained popularity worldwide due to its unique taste and probiotic properties. Beyond being enjoyed as a refreshing drink, kombucha has found its way into various culinary creations across different cultures, including Africa. In this article, we will delve into the fascinating world of kombucha-infused dishes in African cuisine. From ancient traditions to modern fusion recipes, explore the diverse uses of kombucha across the African continent.

1. Equatorial East Africa: Kombucha Marinated Grilled Fish

Originating from coastal regions such as Kenya and Tanzania, kombucha-marinated grilled fish enhances the taste and tenderness in this popular seafood dish. Follow this simple recipe for a burst of flavorful delight:

Ingredients:

- Fresh fish fillets (Tilapia or Nile perch work well)

- Kombucha of your choice (preferably plain or mildly flavored)

- Fresh herbs (such as lemon grass, coriander, and thyme)

- Salt and pepper (to taste)

- Lemon wedges (for garnish)

Instructions:

1. Marinate the fish fillets in kombucha for 30 minutes to infuse flavor and break down potential fish odor.

2. Preheat the grill or barbecue.

3. Sprinkle herbs, salt, and pepper on both sides of the marinated fish.

4. Grill the fish until the flesh is cooked thoroughly and the skin is crispy.

5. Serve the fish with lemon wedges, garnished with fresh herbs.

2. North African Medley: Kombucha Couscous Salad

Couscous is a versatile grain dish found in many African cuisines. Infuse it with a tangy twist by incorporating kombucha. Add this refreshing dish to your Mediterranean-inspired menu:

Ingredients:

- 1 cup couscous, cooked and cooled

- 1 cup finely chopped vegetables (cucumber, tomatoes, bell peppers, red onions)

- Fresh herbs (parsley, mint, or cilantro, to taste)

- Lemon vinaigrette (olive oil, lemon juice, salt, and pepper)

- Kombucha pulp or strained kombucha vinegar (for added tanginess)

- Optional toppings: chickpeas, feta cheese, or olives

Instructions:

1. In a large mixing bowl, combine cooked couscous, vegetables, and herbs.

2. Prepare the lemon vinaigrette by whisking together olive oil, lemon juice, salt, and pepper.

3. Pour the vinaigrette onto the couscous mixture and toss well to ensure even coating.

4. Gently fold kombucha pulp or a drizzle of strained kombucha vinegar into the salad for extra flavor.

5. Add toppings of your choice and refrigerate for at least an hour to enhance flavors before serving.

3. Southern Africa Sensation: Kombucha-Braised Chicken Stew

With aromas inspired by traditional African spices, this kombucha-infused chicken stew is a true southern delight. It brings vibrancy to your taste buds, commemorating the culinary legacies of South Africa and beyond.

Ingredients:

- 1 whole chicken, cut into pieces

- Kombucha of your choice (preferably richly flavored)

- Onion, finely chopped

- Garlic and ginger paste

- Curry powder, ground cumin, paprika (to taste)

- Tomato paste

- Chicken broth or water

- Fresh herbs (such as thyme and bay leaves)

- Salt and pepper (to taste)

Instructions:

1. Brown the chicken pieces in a large pot over medium-high heat.

2. Add onions, garlic, and ginger paste, sautéing until fragrant.

3. Sprinkle curry powder, cumin, paprika, salt, and pepper on the chicken, giving it a gentle stir.

4. Mix in tomato paste, kombucha, broth/water, and herbs, ensuring the chicken is well-coated.

5. Bring to a simmer and cook on low heat until chicken is tender and flavors are fully incorporated.

6. Serve with steamed rice, mashed vegetables, or a crusty bread roll.

THESE EXAMPLES PROVIDE a glimpse into how kombucha has fused with diverse African cuisines to create unique and tantalizing dishes. From the coast of Equatorial East Africa to the shores of North Africa and the heartland of Southern Africa, kombucha experimentation is igniting adventurous culinary journeys across the continent. So, go ahead, embrace the mystique and versatility of kombucha and explore your own kombucha-infused dishes that celebrate Africa's rich culinary heritage.

Chapter 19: Future and Innovation- The current trends and issues of pickles and fermented foods in Africa

Pickles and fermented foods have been an essential part of African cuisine for centuries. With their unique flavors, extended shelf life, and added health benefits, pickles and fermented foods continue to be popular among African communities. In this chapter, we will explore the current trends and issues surrounding pickles and fermented foods in Africa, highlighting their role in the future of African cuisine and innovation.

1. Emergence of Indigenous Fermented Foods:

A notable current trend is the revival and recognition of indigenous fermented foods in Africa. With increased interest in traditional culinary practices, consumers are rediscovering the unique fermented foods, such as coucou and peacehungue from Nigeria, ikivunde from Rwanda, and chibwantu from Zambia. This trend not only promotes cultural preservation but also drives economic growth by utilizing locally available resources.

2. Nutritional Value and Health Benefits:

The growing emphasis on healthy eating has led to an increased interest in the nutritional value and health benefits of pickles and fermented foods. Fermented products such as ogi, a traditional Nigerian fermented cereal, are rich in beneficial bacteria, aiding in gut health. Additionally, pickles made from local vegetables like okra, cucumbers, and carrots offer essential vitamins and fiber. The recognition of these health benefits is driving the consumption of pickles and fermented foods as part of a balanced diet.

3. Innovations and Market Expansion:

Africa is witnessing a rise in innovative approaches to the production and consumption of pickles and fermented foods. Start-ups and food entrepreneurs are introducing new flavors and modern packaging techniques, making these products more accessible to consumers. This innovative mindset has paved the way for market expansion, with African pickles and fermented foods being exported to global markets. Moreover, online platforms and social media are empowering local producers by connecting them with a wider customer base.

4. Quality Control and Standardization:

One of the critical issues faced by the pickle and fermented food industry in Africa is the lack of quality control and standardization. As the demand for these products grows, ensuring consistency and safety becomes paramount. Collaborative efforts between stakeholders, such as governments, health agencies, and food manufacturers, are necessary to establish quality standards, regulations, and certification systems. These initiatives will not only protect consumers but also boost exports and economic growth.

5. Climate Change Adaptation:

Climate change poses a challenge to the production of pickles and fermented foods in Africa. Agricultural practices, such as growing seasonal vegetables and herbs used in traditional pickling processes, are threatened by unpredictable weather patterns and declining soil fertility. Adaptation strategies, such as promoting sustainable farming practices, diversifying crop varieties, and investing in climate-resilient infrastructure, will be crucial to ensuring a consistent supply of raw materials for the industry.

⎯⎯⎯◦⎯⎯⎯

PICKLES AND FERMENTED foods hold immense potential for the future of African cuisine. The current trends of reviving indigenous foods, recognizing their health benefits, and promoting innovation present exciting opportunities for local producers and entrepreneurs. However, addressing issues related to quality control, standardization, and climate change adaptation will be essential in harnessing the full potential of pickles and fermented foods in Africa. By embracing these challenges, Africa can position itself as a global leader in this vibrant and culturally significant industry.

- The prospects and challenges of pickles and fermented foods in Africa

The Prospects and Challenges of Pickles and Fermented Foods in Africa

PICKLES AND FERMENTED foods have been a part of human culture and cuisine for thousands of years. They not only enhance the flavor of meals but also provide numerous health benefits. In recent years, there has been a resurgence in the popularity of these traditional foods due to their unique taste profiles and perceived health advantages. This article explores the prospects and challenges of pickles and fermented foods in Africa, examining their potential growth and contribution to the African culinary landscape.

Prospects of Pickles and Fermented Foods in Africa

1. Cultural Significance:

Africa is an incredibly diverse continent with numerous cultural and culinary traditions. Many African communities have a long-standing history of pickling and fermenting various foods, such as vegetables, fruits, and legumes. These foods are deeply rooted in African culture and offer an opportunity for preserving culinary heritage while embracing future food trends.

2. Economic Opportunities:

The global market for pickles and fermented foods has witnessed a significant increase in recent years, creating economic opportunities for African countries. With their diverse climates and rich agricultural resources, Africa has the potential to become a hub for producing and exporting a wide range of pickled and fermented products. This can lead to the creation of jobs and increased revenue for local communities.

3. Nutritional Benefits:

Pickles and fermented foods are not only delicious but also offer several health benefits. Fermentation enhances the bioavailability of nutrients, making them more easily absorbable by the body. African populations, facing malnutrition challenges, can greatly benefit from incorporating these nutritious foods into their diets. The abundance of local fruits, vegetables, and grains in Africa can contribute to the production of unique and highly nutritious fermented products.

Challenges of Pickles and Fermented Foods in Africa

1. Limited awareness and accessibility:

One of the challenges faced by pickles and fermented foods in Africa is limited awareness among the population. The majority of African consumers are not familiar with the health benefits and range of flavors offered by these products. Educational campaigns and marketing strategies are required to create awareness and promote the consumption of pickles and fermented foods.

2. Lack of infrastructure for large-scale production:

The absence of proper infrastructure and technical know-how poses a significant challenge for the large-scale production of pickles and fermented foods. The fermentation process requires precise temperature control, hygienic conditions, and adequate storage facilities. Developing countries in Africa need to invest in food processing facilities and provide training to farmers and processors to ensure quality production.

3. Variability in consumer preferences:

Africa encompasses diverse cultures and taste preferences. Multiple regions within the continent have unique styles of pickling and fermenting foods. This variability in tastes and preferences can pose a challenge for commercializing these products across the entire African continent. Producers need to adapt their recipes and product offerings to cater to the specific demands of different regions.

Conclusion

The prospects for the growth and popularity of pickles and fermented foods in Africa are high. Leveraging cultural significance, economic opportunities, and nutritional benefits can propel these traditional foods into the mainstream. Addressing the challenges through awareness campaigns, infrastructure development, and product customization will be crucial for advancing the proliferation of pickles and fermented foods throughout the continent. By doing so, Africa can embrace its culinary heritage while contributing to the global trend of sustainable and nutritious food choices.

- The role of pickles and fermented foods in the vision and action of African futures

The Role of Pickles and Fermented Foods in the Vision and Action of African Futures

———◦———

IN RECENT YEARS, THERE has been a growing global trend towards valuing traditional and natural food preservation methods, especially concerning pickles and fermented foods. These indigenous practices can be traced throughout the span of human civilization across various continents. This article aims to shed light on the underrated but crucial role of pickles and fermented foods in shaping the vision and action of African futures. From the cultural significance to the health benefits, these foods hold immense potential in promoting sustainability, economic growth, and national identity in African nations.

1. Cultural Significance:

Pickles and fermented foods find their roots deep in the African culture and history, being an integral part of traditional cuisines. Apart from their nutritional value, these foods carry centuries-old traditions and knowledge passed down through generations. Preserving these practices not only preserves cultural heritage but also fosters a sense of community and identity.

2. Economic Opportunities:

The utilization, production, and promotion of pickles and fermented foods can create tremendous economic opportunities for African countries. The production and sale of these products can serve as small-scale cottage industries, supporting local communities and contributing to grassroots developments. Moreover, with increasing demand and recognition in international markets due to the rising popularity of natural food products, African nations can tap into the export potential of pickles and fermented foods to boost their economies.

3. Health Benefits:

Pickles and fermented foods offer numerous health benefits due to their unique fermentation process. Lactic acid fermentation of these foods leads to enhanced bioavailability of nutrients and the production of beneficial probiotics. This promotes healthy gut microbiota, strengthens the immune system, and reduces the risk of chronic diseases such as obesity, diabetes, and cardiovascular diseases. By actively promoting the consumption of these traditional foods, African nations can address health challenges and improve the overall well-being of their populations.

4. Environmental Sustainability:

In an era of increasing concern about the impact of food production on the environment, pickles and fermented foods present a sustainable and eco-friendly solution. These food preservation methods not only reduce food waste but also minimize energy consumption, the need for refrigeration, and resource depletion. By embracing traditional preservation techniques, African societies can contribute to sustainable development goals by conserving resources and reducing their ecological footprint.

5. Social Impact and Food Security:

Promoting the consumption and production of pickles and fermented foods can have a significant impact on food security in Africa. Their long shelf life, affordability, and ability to utilize surplus produce help alleviate food scarcity. Additionally, the revival of traditional preservation techniques can empower communities, encouraging self-sufficiency and equity in the food system. By incorporating these foods into national food policies, African nations can take a decisive step towards ensuring food security for its people.

⊙

THE INCORPORATION OF pickles and fermented foods into the vision and action of African futures holds great promise, showcasing cultural heritage, fostering economic growth, improving public health, driving environmental sustainability, and addressing food security challenges. It is imperative for policy-makers, researchers, and civil society to recognize and support the value of these traditional practices. By doing so, African nations can unlock their potential and leverage the richness of their gastronomic heritage to shape a brighter and more prosperous future.

Conclusion

In conclusion, this book has delved deep into a myriad of topics, exploring various issues and presenting a wealth of information to the reader. Throughout its pages, the author has meticulously detailed numerous findings and arguments, providing an in-depth analysis of the subject matter.

One of the main findings highlighted in this book is the impact of social media on society. The author discusses how platforms like Facebook, Instagram, and Twitter have transformed communication, making it easier for people to connect and share their thoughts and experiences. However, the book also delves into the darker side of social media, such as its role in perpetuating negative body image or facilitating cyberbullying. By synthesizing different viewpoints and research studies, the author offers a comprehensive understanding of this ever-evolving socio-technological phenomenon.

Another prominent argument explored in this book is the increasing influence of artificial intelligence (AI) and automation in various fields. The author examines the benefits of AI-driven technologies, such as increased efficiency in industries like healthcare or logistics. However, the book also raises concerns about the potential labor market disruption caused by automation. By presenting contrasting perspectives and supported arguments, the author urges readers to consider the implications of a world increasingly reliant on AI.

Furthermore, this book touches upon the pressing issue of climate change. The author delves into scientific research and statistical data to underline the severity of the situation. From melting ice caps to rising temperatures, the evidence presented paints a stark picture of the consequences humanity might face if we do not take immediate action. The book also catalogues various attempts at mitigating climate change, providing readers with a sense of hope and encouraging them to adopt sustainable practices.

Overall, this book successfully synthesizes the main findings and arguments discussed into a comprehensive and engaging narrative. Its attention to detail and wide-ranging scope make it a valuable resource for anyone seeking a deeper understanding of the topics at hand. As a reader, one cannot help but appreciate the author's effort to present objective information and incorporate differing opinions. This book challenges readers to critically analyze the complexities of contemporary issues and empowers them to form educated opinions. Whether you agree or disagree with the presented arguments, this book undeniably succeeds in stimulating intellectual discourse and raising awareness on important societal matters.

The Implications and Contributions of a Book to the Field of Food Studies and African Studies

———◦———

FOOD HAS ALWAYS PLAYED a crucial role in shaping cultural identities, economic systems, and social structures. Therefore, understanding food practices in different regions offers significant insights into the complexities of human societies. In this context, the implications and contributions of a book focusing on food studies in Africa hold particular relevance. Such a book has the potential to advance research and understanding in both the field of food studies and African studies. This essay aims to explore the lengthy, detailed, and fascinating information found within such a book, discussing its broader implications and contributions to these two fields.

Implications for Food Studies:

1. Cultural identities and traditions:

The book delves into the diverse food cultures found in Africa, deepening our understanding of how different nations and ethnic groups' food practices contribute to the formation of their cultural identities. By exploring the origins, rituals, and symbolism connected to various African foodways, the book enriches the discourse on cultural studies within the field of food studies.

2. Culinary history and evolution:

By delving into the historical origins of African food practices, the book uncovers the impact of colonization, trade, and migration on the continent's culinary traditions. It offers a valuable resource for scholars interested in tracing the evolution of African cuisines and their integration into global culinary landscapes.

3. Sustainable food systems and agrarian practices:

Exploring the traditional and modern agrarian practices in Africa, the book sheds light on the continent's striving for sustainable and resilient food systems. By addressing issues related to climate change, land access, and the preservation of biodiversity, the book provides valuable insights for researchers and policymakers working on food security and rural development.

Contributions to African Studies:

1. Social dynamics and gender roles:

The book uncovers how food practices in Africa are intricately linked to social dynamics, gender roles, and power structures. In analyzing the division of labor, culinary symbolism, and food sharing practices, it offers a valuable contribution to African studies by examining how food intersects with broader societal structures.

2. Economic implications and global interactions:

Bridging the gap between food studies and African studies, the book highlights the economic implications of African foodways on local markets, trading networks, and global encounters. It explores patterns of agricultural production, export-oriented economies, and the impact of multinational food corporations on African consumers and markets.

3. Political and health considerations:

Food is inherently linked to political discussions, particularly regarding resource allocation, nutrition policies, and public health concerns. The book investigates how food has been both a catalyst and a conduit for political transformation in Africa. It addresses issues like food security, food sovereignty, and the impact of globalization on local diets, contributing to broader discussions within African studies.

IN CONCLUSION, A DETAILED and comprehensive book on food studies in Africa holds significant implications and contributions to both the field of food studies and African studies. By examining the rich tapestry of cultural, economic, and social aspects surrounding African foodways, the book enhances our understanding of the complexities inherent within diverse societies. The insights gained from such an exploration can support scholars and policymakers in fostering sustainable food systems, preserving cultural heritage, and promoting equitable development in Africa.

- The suggestions and recommendations for further research and exploration on African pickles and fermented foods

Exploring the Untapped Potential of African Pickles and Fermented Foods: Suggestions for Further Research and Exploration

AFRICAN CUISINE IS renowned for its rich flavors and diverse culinary traditions. One aspect that often goes unnoticed, despite its significance, is the wide variety of traditional African pickles and fermented foods. These gastronomic treasures hold great potential not only for the culinary world but also for their nutritional value and socioeconomic impact. However, there is a lack of comprehensive research on African pickles and fermented foods. This article aims to suggest areas for further investigation and exploration to unveil the untapped potential of these unique products.

1. Botanical and Cultural Diversity:

African pickles and fermented foods are influenced by the enormous diversity of crops and indigenous knowledge across the continent. Further research is needed to identify and document various African plants, vegetables, fruits, tubers, and grains used in pickling and fermentation processes. Exploring different African communities and their specifics recipes, techniques, and cultural practices related to these traditional foods will provide valuable insight into the diversity and cultural significance of this culinary tradition.

2. Nutritional Profiling:

A comprehensive understanding of the nutritional composition of African pickles and fermented foods is essential. Conducting studies that evaluate the specific changes in nutrients during the fermentation process, including the production/release of bioactive compounds, can provide insight into the potential health benefits associated with these foods. There is also a need for comparative nutritional analyses of different types of African pickles as well as assessments of their shelf life and safety.

3. Medicinal and Health-Promoting Properties:

Many African pickles and fermented foods have been traditionally associated with various health benefits. Investigations into their medicinal properties, including antimicrobial, antioxidative, and anti-inflammatory activities, could provide valuable insights into their potential for use as functional foods or nutraceuticals. Further research can also focus on identifying specific strains of bacteria or yeasts responsible for fermentation and their potential probiotic qualities.

4. Economic and Socioeconomic Implications:

Examining the socioeconomic impact of African pickles and fermented foods is crucial for realizing their full potential. Research can focus on understanding the traditional methods of production, processing, and marketing, and exploring ways to strengthen value chains and promote these products locally and globally. Additionally, such investigations can shed light on the socio-cultural and economic roles of women, who often play a significant role in the production and preservation of these foods.

5. Culinary Applications and Innovation:

African pickles and fermented foods have immense culinary potential and can be integrated into various dishes and cuisines worldwide. Further exploration can include recipe development and experimentation with these traditional products across different culinary contexts. Partnerships among researchers, chefs, and culinary institutes can facilitate the creative integration of these flavors, promoting African gastronomy and broadening culinary traditions globally.

6. Technological Innovations:

Research should explore the development and refinement of efficient and sustainable technologies for the production of African pickles and fermented foods. Preservation techniques, such as optimization of fermentation parameters (temperature, time, moisture, pH control), standardized packaging, and food safety, need exploration to enhance commercial viability at both small-scale and industrial levels. Modern tools like food biotechnology, genetic studies, and novel packaging techniques should also be employed for improved quality and consumer acceptability.

THE EXPLORATION AND understanding of African pickles and fermented foods have only begun to scratch the surface of their culinary, nutritional, and socioeconomic potential. Further interdisciplinary research and collaboration among African food scientists, nutritionists, botanists, anthropologists, and culinary experts are crucial. Unveiling the secrets of these fascinating ethnic delights will undoubtedly cement their status as iconic African gastronomic assets, offer new health opportunities, and promote sustainability within local communities and beyond.